D0758213

PIONEERS
IN
MODERN FACTORY MANAGEMENT

This is a volume in the
Arno Press collection

HISTORY OF MANAGEMENT THOUGHT

Advisory Editors
Kenneth E. Carpenter
Alfred D. Chandler

Consulting Editor
Stuart Bruchey

See last pages of this volume
for a complete list of titles

PIONEERS
IN
MODERN FACTORY MANAGEMENT

Edited by
Alfred D. Chandler

ARNO PRESS
A New York Times Company
New York • 1979

Publisher's Note: This book has been reproduced from the best available copy.

Editorial Supervision: BRIAN QUINN
Reprint Edition 1979 by Arno Press Inc.

HISTORY OF MANAGEMENT THOUGHT
  AND PRACTICE
ISBN for complete set: 0-405-12306-X
See last pages of this volume for titles.

Manufactured in the United States of America

Library of Congress Cataloging in Publication Data
Main entry under title:

Pioneers in modern factory management.

(History of management thought)
Reprint of papers originally presented at the annual meetings of the American Society of Mechanical Engineers and published in the Society's Transactions, 1885-95.
    1. Factory management--Addresses, essays, lectures.
I. Chandler, Alfred Dupont. II. American Society of Mechanical Engineers. Transactions. III. Series.
TS155.P486 1979   658'.008   79-7526
ISBN 0-405-12310-8

CONTENTS

THE ENGINEER
AS AN ECONOMIST

Henry R. Towne

CCVII.

THE ENGINEER AS AN ECONOMIST.

BY HENRY R. TOWNE, STAMFORD, CONN.

THE monogram of our national initials, which is the symbol for our monetary unit, the dollar, is almost as frequently conjoined to the figures of an engineer's calculations as are the symbols indicating feet, minutes, pounds, or gallons. The final issue of his work, in probably a majority of cases, resolves itself into a question of dollars and cents, of relative or absolute values. This statement, while true in regard to the work of all engineers, applies particularly to that of the mechanical engineer, for the reason that his functions, more frequently than in the case of others, include the executive duties of organizing and superintending the operations of industrial establishments, and of directing the labor of the artisans whose organized efforts yield the fruition of his work.

To insure the best results, the organization of productive labor must be directed and controlled by persons having not only good executive ability, and possessing the practical familiarity of a mechanic or engineer with the goods produced and the processes employed, but having also, and equally, a practical knowledge of how to observe, record, analyze and compare essential facts in relation to wages, supplies, expense accounts, and all else that enters into or affects the economy of production and the cost of the product. There are many good mechanical engineers;—there are also many good " business men;"—but the two are rarely combined in one person. But this combination of qualities, together with at least some skill as an accountant, either in one person or more, is essential to the successful management of industrial works, and has its highest effectiveness if united in one person, who is thus qualified to supervise, either personally or through assistants, the operations of all departments of a business, and to subordinate each to the harmonious development of the whole.

Engineering has long been conceded a place as one of the modern arts, and has become a well-defined science, with a large and growing literature of its own, and of late years has subdivided itself into numerous and distinct divisions, one of which is that of mechanical engineering. It will probably not be disputed that the matter of shop management is of equal importance with that of engineering, as affecting the successful conduct of most, if not all, of our great industrial establishments, and that the *management of works* has become a matter of such great and far-reaching importance as perhaps to justify its classification also as one of the modern arts. The one is a well-defined science, with a distinct literature, with numerous journals and with many associations for the interchange of experience; the other is unorganized, is almost without literature, has no organ or medium for the interchange of experience, and is without association or organization of any kind. A vast amount of accumulated experience in the art of workshop management already exists, but there is no record of it available to the world in general, and each old enterprise is managed more or less in its own way, receiving little benefit from the parallel experience of other similar enterprises, and imparting as little of its own to them; while each new enterprise, starting *de novo* and with much labor, and usually at much cost for experience, gradually develops a more or less perfect system of its own, according to the ability of its managers, receiving little benefit or aid from all that may have been done previously by others in precisely the same field of work.

Surely this condition of things is wrong and should be remedied. But the remedy must not be looked for from those who are " business men " or clerks and accountants only; it should come from those whose training and experience has given them an understanding of both sides (viz.: the mechanical and the clerical) of the important questions involved. It should originate, therefore, from those who are also engineers, and, for the reasons above indicated, particularly from mechanical engineers. Granting this, why should it not originate from, and be promoted by The American Society of Mechanical Engineers ?

To consider this proposition more definitely, let us state the work which requires to be done. The questions to be considered, and which need recording and publication as conducing to discussion and the dissemination of useful knowledge in this specialty, group themselves under two principal heads, namely: Shop Management, and Shop Accounting. A third head may be named which is subordinate to, and partly included in each of these, namely: Shop Forms and Blanks. Under the head of Shop Management fall the questions of organization, responsibility, reports, systems of contract and piece work, and all that relates to the executive management of works, mills and factories. Under the head of Shop Accounting fall the questions of time and wages systems, determination of costs, whether by piece or day-work, the distribution of the various expense accounts, the ascertainment of profits, methods of book-keeping, and all that enters into the system of accounts which relates to the manufacturing departments of a business, and to the determination and record of its results.

There already exists an enormous fund of information relating to such matters, based upon actual and most extensive experience. What is now needed is a medium for the interchange of this experience among those whom it interests and concerns. Probably no better way for this exists than that obtaining in other instances, namely, by the publication of papers and reports, and by meetings for the discussion of papers and interchange of opinions.

The subject thus outlined, however distinct and apart from the primary functions of this society, is, nevertheless, germane to the interests of most, if not all, of its members. Conceding this, why should not the functions of the society be so enlarged as to embrace this new field of usefulness? This work, if undertaken, may be kept separate and distinct from the present work of the society by organizing a new "section" (which might be designated the "Economic Section"), the scope of which would embrace all papers and discussions relating to the topics herein referred to. The meetings of this section could be held either separately from, or immediately following the regular meetings of the society, and its papers could appear as a supplement to the regular transactions. In this way all interference would be avoided with the primary and chief business of the society, and the attendance at the meetings of the new section would naturally resolve itself into such portion of the membership as is interested in the objects for which it would be organized.

As a single illustration of the class of subjects to be covered by the discussions and papers of the proposed new section, and of the benefit to be derived therefrom, there may be cited the case of a manufacturing establishment in which there is now in use, in connection with the manufacturing accounts and exclusive of the ordinary commercial accounts, some twenty various forms of special record and account books, and more than one hundred printed forms and blanks. The primary object to which all of these contribute is the systematic recording of the operations of the different departments of the works, and the computation therefrom of such statistical information as is essential to the efficient management of the business, and especially to increased economy of production. All of these special books and forms have been the outgrowth of experience extending over many years, and represent a large amount of thoughtful planning and intelligent effort at constant development and improvement. The methods thus arrived at would un-

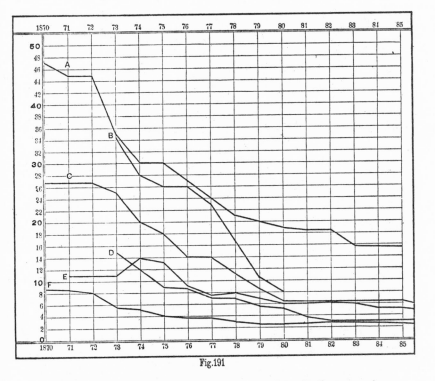

Fig.191

doubtedly be of great value to others engaged in similar operations, and particularly to persons engaged in organizing and starting new enterprises. It is probable that much, if not all, of the information and experience referred to would be willingly made public through such a channel as is herein suggested, particularly if such action on the part of one firm or corporation would be responded to in like manner by others, so that each member could reasonably expect to receive some equivalent for his contributions by the benefit which he would derive from the experience of others.

In the case of the establishment above referred to, a special system of contract and piece-work has been in operation for some fifteen years, the results from which, in reducing the labor cost on certain products without encroaching upon the earnings of the men engaged, have been quite striking. A few of these results, selected at random, are indicated by the accompanying diagram (Fig. 191), the diagonal lines on which represent the fluctuations in the labor cost of certain special products during the time covered by the table, the vertical scale representing values.

Undoubtedly a portion of the reductions thus indicated resulted from improved appliances, larger product, and increased experience, but after making due allowance for all of these, there remains a large portion of the reduction which, to the writer's knowledge, is fairly attributable to the operations of the peculiar piece-work system adopted. The details and operations of this system would probably be placed before the society, in due time, through the channel of the proposed new section, should the latter take definite form. Other, and probably much more valuable, information and experience relating to systems of contract and piece-work would doubtless be contributed by other members, and in the aggregate a great amount of information of a most valuable character would thus be made available to the whole membership of the society.

In conclusion, it is suggested that if the plan herein proposed commends itself favorably to the members present at the meeting at which it is presented, the subject had best be referred to a special committee, by whom it can be carefully considered, and by whom, if it seems expedient to proceed further, the whole matter can be matured and formulated in an orderly manner, and thus be so presented at a future meeting as to enable the society then intelligently to act upon the question, and to decide whether or not to adopt the recommendations made by such committee.

(This paper received discussion in connection with two others on germane topics. The discussion is printed at the end of the paper on " The Shop-Order System of Accounts.")

INVENTORY VALUATION
OF MACHINERY PLANT

Oberlin Smith

CCVIII.

INVENTORY VALUATION OF MACHINERY PLANT.

BY OBERLIN SMITH, BRIDGETON, N. J.

THE keeping of *cost* and *valuation* accounts in connection with machinery has never been brought into so perfect a system as has ordinary commercial book-keeping. Recently, however, there has been a good deal of interest taken in the subject, and new light has been thrown upon keeping *cost* accounts by such valuable books as those of Captain Metcalfe and others. The matter of inventory valuations, however, with which it is proposed briefly to deal in this paper, is, to say the least, in a very mixed up condition, and although with some machinery owners it has received considerable attention, the average method contains a good deal of guesswork.

It is evident that at the very base of all account-keeping is the finding out the true value of the property kept account of ; and that without this being correct, all else is useless.

Probably the most popular and frequently used method of doing this is by pure guessing. Another system is that of taking original cost at first, and then depreciating a given percentage each year, regardless of the several modifying conditions which will be mentioned later on. One large manufacturer, known to the writer, used to work upon this system with his machine tools, depreciating their value 10 per cent. each year.. Although acknowledging that it brought the figures rather too low, he said that it kept him upon the safe side, in not letting his assets appear of greater value than they really were. However safe this method may be, it is worthless if the object is to show the real value of the property. This will be apparent if reference is made to the second line of the following table, wherein $100 is shown decreased at the end of each year 10 per cent. from the remainder belonging to the year previous :

YEAR.	0	1	2	3	4	5	6	7	8	9	10	15	20
10% off	$100.00	$90.00	$81.00	$72.90	$65.61	$59.05	$53.15	$47.83	$43.05	$38.74	$34.87	$20.59	$12.16
5% off	100.00	95.00	90.25	85.74	81.45	77.38	73.51	69.83	66 34	63.03	59.88	46.33	35.85

28

It will be noticed that at the end of 10 years the amount is only about 35 dollars, at the end of 15 years 20½ dollars, and at the end of 20 years about 12 dollars. In the third line is shown the respective amounts for $100 as depreciated 5 per cent. each year instead of 10. This gives about $60, $46, and $36 respectively, as the amounts at the end of 10, 15, and 20 years, and it is much more reasonable, for the valuation of machine tools, than is the first mentioned discount, if a system of this kind, with a constant ratio, is to be employed at all. The absurdity is, however, apparent, of using a tool costing $100 when in such bad condition as to be worth but $12, or even $36. Such practice would be suicidal; and yet many tools need not be thrown away in 20 years.

Another method is to estimate the probable price which an article would bring at auction. This is a very indefinite way, as it is well known that there are auctions *and* auctions. In some of these the property brings more than it is really worth, while in others, where the proper bidders do not happen to be present, or where an article is bought for a purpose for which it is unfit, the prices are sometimes almost *nil*.

A striking illustration of the variable values which may be attached to a lot of plant may be seen by comparing the average insurance value and the average taxation value, the latter being usually a very different thing from the former, and the difference being something that frequently sadly puzzles the conscience of the owner to adjust, as it is a soothing balm to his pocket-book. The system now used of taxing machine-shop plant is very variable, and the average tax-assessor is often at his wits' end to know what value to put upon such articles as patterns and special tools, even if he arrives at any fair conclusion regarding the standard machinery. The result is usually a compromise between the high guesses of the assessor and the low guesses of the owner.

It will not be necessary in this paper to dwell upon the best methods of finding the cost of machinery or its productions, but taking it for granted that a machine shop's accountants have a complete record of the cost of all its plant, whether it shall have been purchased or made upon the premises, and supposing further that said plant is new and not deteriorated by wear, the question arises what is its *value?* The first and most important thing to do is for everybody concerned to get it out of their heads that value is necessarily dependent upon cost. There are many modifying conditions which prevent this being true. First among these variable conditions is commercial *fluctuation* of value, and this applies perhaps more to purchased articles, such as standard machine tools bought in open market, than to patterns and other special tools, etc., made upon the premises ; although the latter classes have of course certain fluctuations in cost, dependent upon the labor market and the current price of materials. Thus, if an engine lathe should have been purchased a year ago for $1,000, and remaining unused, should now be assessed, its value, of course, would depend upon the present price charged by its maker. A second factor in variation of values is *locality*. For instance, if the lathe above spoken of was to be used in a mountainous region away from railroads, it would be fair to add to its value at that place the freight and other expenses (perhaps also custom duties) paid to get it there, providing an equally good and cheap lathe could not be bought nearer at hand, where the freight would be less in amount. An appraiser must, however, be careful not to follow the rule of adding freight and custom charges to the cost of a machine, without proper discrimination as to whether it was necessary to bring the tool from a great distance or from a foreign country, instead of buying something nearer at hand. If the latter could have been done, the whole of such charges should of course not be added.

A third variable pertaining to values is *obsoleteness*, for it is evident that our hypothetical $1,000 lathe, even if it has been bought at the lowest market price, which has not yet fallen ; and near at hand, where no freight of much amount was to be added ; and is new and in perfect condition, is not worth $1,000 if a lathe can be bought for the same price which is of such superior design that twice as much work can be done with it in a given time. In this case, the first-mentioned lathe is practically obsolete, and its value might be less than nothing. This supposable case is, of course, an extreme one, but the fact is that in these days of intense inventive activity, machinery is constantly becoming more or less obsolete. In many cases, this is so only to a slight degree, especially in cases of machine tools, such as lathes, planers, drill-presses, etc. This fact is not much to the credit of mechanical engineers, but it is nevertheless a fact, that far less original design has been put into this class of tools than into many others outside of machine shops.

A fourth, and the most obvious cause of depreciation in machinery plant, is *wear and tear*, and there is perhaps more good judgment necessary in determining the exact amount of this depreciation than in any other part of the appraiser's work.

The grand principle which lies at the root of correct valuation, and which should govern the appraiser throughout all his work, is, that any article is worth not what it *did cost*, but *what it would cost to replace it to-day*, providing it is so useful that it would be desirable to so replace it were it destroyed. Thus, if a shop has a lot of machine tools which are built so near to the best modern practice that it would be desirable to duplicate them were they destroyed, they are worth exactly what said duplicates would now cost delivered and set up in the shop, less the depreciation due to the wear and tear. This rule also applies to boilers, engines, shafting, belting, shop fixtures, and small tools—anything, in fact, which can be bought in open market (and, for that matter, it can be applied also to buildings and ground, as well as plant). In the case of working drawings, patterns for castings, and other special tools, such as jigs, etc., all of which are usually made upon the premises, and whose chief cost consists in the items of labor and general expenses, together with a small amount for material, the method of obtaining the true value is of course somewhat more complicated. This is for the reason that the amount which such an article did cost is a very poor index of what it would cost to build a second one, it being usually the case that but one of a kind is needed, and no duplicate has been made. There must necessarily be some guess-work in getting the value of these articles, but it is usually from 10 to 30 per cent. less than the original cost spoken of—that is, if in full use. With this class of tools, the variation of market-price, locality, and wear and tear, do not occur to so great an extent as with machine tools proper, but the variation due to obsoleteness occurs in a very much greater degree than with almost any other class of property. It will be noticed above that working drawings and patterns are classed with jigs, as " special tools." They are not always regarded as such, but undoubtedly should be, as they have exactly the same general conditions governing their use. It may be here said that a marked distinction should always be made between an original drawing and a working drawing. One of the former class may cost $1,000 to make, on account of the designing which is incorporated with it, but as a drawing it is not worth more than $10, if it can be duplicated by an ordinary journeyman draughtsman for that amount. Whatever value the designing spoken of has in itself, must be found in some other part of the inventory, under the head of " patent rights," " good will," or something of that kind, rather than in the class " drawings." A working drawing, therefore, is (and the same way with a jig) worth exactly what it would cost for a draughtsman to copy it off, plus the paper on which it is drawn. A pattern is worth exactly what the wages and general expenses would be for a pattern maker to duplicate it, plus cost of the wood, glue, varnish, or other material. The true value of a jig or templet may obviously be found in the same manner, always assuming that said articles are needed for frequent use in the regular production of the goods manufactured by the shop in question. It is evident that the value of all these classes of special tools depreciates enormously if said production is permanently decreased from regular and standard to occasional, or if the articles made are.going out of fashion in the market, or are not able to compete in price with others of a similar nature. If they have become entirely unsalable from the above causes, or from having been superseded by improved articles of some other kind, then the value of the drawings, patterns, and other special tools with which they were produced is of course reduced to nothing. Great care should always be taken in appraising to rate such articles low enough so as not to show deceptively high assets, but at the same time, in justice to all concerned in the ownership of the property, they should not be put at a foolishly low figure, as were the patterns of a large manufacturing concern known to the writer, whose policy was to gradually depreciate all their patterns, until their value stood at "nothing" upon their books. This of course made them safe against showing false profits, and also had the merit of making their inventory worthless for this particular class of tools, as far as the legitimate functions of an inventory are concerned. The simplicity and ingenuity of this plan was more conspicuous than its common sense, especially after some time had elapsed, and the figures had gotten down very low. Of course if the system was right at this time, it must have been wrong at first, and to carry it out logically the patterns should all have been counted as worth nothing when they were first made.

In all jobbing machine shops, which do repairing and odd work rather than limiting themselves to standard manufacturing, there is a large accumulation of drawings and patterns (not usually, however, many jigs), which belong to what may be called "transient" jobs, and which will probably never be used again, or at any rate only occasionally. These should be valued at a very low figure, usually less than 10 per cent. of what they cost, the amount of this percentage depending upon the probabilities of their future use.

In estimating the depreciation due to wear and tear in engines, shafting, belting and machine tools, due regard should be had to the general system upon which they are run—whether they are allowed to wear themselves almost entirely out and are then replaced by new ones, of which a new inventory is taken, or whether they are kept up to a certain standard of goodness by the replacing of worn parts, etc. The latter is the system practiced by the writer for many years past, and is, in his opinion, undoubtedly the best one. Leaving out the question of *obsoleteness*, there is no reason why a lathe or a planer should not be run for twenty or thirty years and kept up to the standard (by frequent repairs and replacement of parts) to which it has attained in the third or fourth year of its age. Shafting and pulleys can be regarded in the same way, but can probably be kept nearer to a new standard, as they do not wear out so fast. Belting also can be treated upon the same principle, but kept at a lower standard, the average condition of a lot of belting throughout a shop usually being probably nearly half worn-out. The writer intends, for his own use, to establish for these classes of machinery, and also for small tools, such as twist drills, reamers, etc., a standard percentage of "worn-outness"—if such a word may be coined for the occasion. He has not yet made an accurate estimate of the proper percentage to be employed in each case, but probably a fair allowance for the percentage of present new value in a well equipped and properly taken care of machine shop (leaving out, as before intimated, the question of obsoleteness), would be, for shafting, etc., 80 to 90 per cent., engines and machine tools, 70 to 80 per cent., boilers and belting, 60 to 70 per cent., and small tools (which are constanly being ground away), 50 to 60 per cent. This estimate is, of course, only approximate, and its correctness would vary with the standard of condition which was adopted and the consequent thoroughness and frequency of repairs.

A properly kept inventory of the class of articles just mentioned would put them at new value the first year, and depreciate them from 5 to 10 per cent. annually, until the standard *constant* was reached, after which they would remain at about the same price each year, except as affected by violent fluctuations in the market, and by obsoleteness of design.

With regard to the special tools before mentioned, the depreciation for wear and tear need be but very little, as if they serve their purpose at all, they must be kept in such repair as to serve it perfectly; and they are not a marketable article in which a slight deterioration in appearance would largely affect their value, as would be the case with standard articles. In the case of working-drawings, which are usually of trifling value, it is not worth while to take account of the wear and tear, as when worn too much for use they can be wholly replaced with duplicates, and the valuation can be kept, for convenience, at the same rate.

An excellent mental aid to an appraiser, in considering the value of doubtful articles, is to estimate what he would be willing to bid at auction for a duplicate, were the article destroyed. This amount, if correctly guessed at, is certainly a true index of the real value.

The writer has for several years past paid considerable attention to keeping a systematic inventory, in which all the property of the machine works with which he is connected is classified into "classes" and "sub-classes," so entered in tabular form that the names need not be re-written yearly except in case of additional articles entered. In this book there is a set of columns provided for each year, for a term of years to come, so that the value merely need be entered, together with the amount of depreciation since the last year. There are proper columns provided for cost, variation therefrom to obtain actual new value, subsequent depreciation for the various causes that have been mentioned in this paper, etc., etc. He will not, however, occupy the time of the Society now to describe this book in detail, though it may possibly furnish a theme for some future occasion. The object of this paper will be attained if it shall haply influence even a few among many engineers to us more systematic methods in estimating the true value of the property in their charge.

As a recapitulation of the foregoing, the rules governing an appraiser may be tersely stated thus: Rate all property that it would be desirable to reproduce, were it destroyed to-day, at the net cost of such reproduction, in its existing locality, minus its estimated damage by wear and tear. Rate partially obsolete articles the same way, but minus also a percentage of their apparent value equal to their estimated percentage of obsoleteness or of improbability of usefulness. Rate wholly obsolete articles at nothing.

(*This paper was read in connection with the paper on " The Shop-Order System of Accounts," and the discussion is printed at the close of the latter.*)

THE SHOP-ORDER SYSTEM
OF
ACCOUNTS AND DISCUSSION

Henry Metcalfe

CCIX

THE SHOP-ORDER SYSTEM OF ACCOUNTS.

BY HENRY METCALFE, WATERVLIET ARSENAL, TROY, N. Y.

I.

Let us imagine the art of music before its notation was devised. Think of the strains which might have been immortal, but which died as voices die, and were lost. Imagine the energy wasted in repetition: the effort beginning afresh with each new learner of each new tune, enlarging his own experience merely and leaving no vestige to guide another's way.

Look forward, on the other hand, and imagine it possible to catch and fix the vibrations of an untrammeled voice seeking expression in speech or song. Is not this the ideal toward which stenography and phonography are but instinctive and feeble approaches?

Now, administration without records is like music without notes —by ear. Good as far as it goes—which is but a little way—it bequeathes nothing to the future. Except in the very rudest industries, carried on as if from hand to mouth, all recognize that the present must prepare for the demands of the future, and hence records, more or less elaborate, are kept. Their elaboration depends on what their results are worth.

I used to think that only government workshops suffered from circumlocution, and took it for granted that private establishments had simple and direct methods of procuring supplies, of keeping track of work in progress and of determining its cost when done. I knew, of course, that no shop running to make money could afford to wait, as I have had to do, for the most necessary material, and assumed that in other respects their management was generally on a par with their facility in procuring supplies.

But in seeking better methods where the permanent personal responsibility of profit tends to whittle off excrescences of administration which lead to wasteful delay, I found that much had been sacrificed to immediate advantage; that records were too often kept by memory, so that as the manager of an establishment employing 1,400 men once told me, " The trouble is, not in fore-seeing necessities, nor in starting the work to meet them ; but in constantly running over the back track to see that nothing ordered has been overlooked, and in settling disputes as to whether such and such an order was or was not actually given and received. Super-intendence," said he, " would be very different work if I were sure that an order once given would go of itself through the works, leav-ing a permanent trail by which I could follow it and decide posi-tively where and by whom it was stopped. As it is, I spend so much of my time in 'shooing' along my orders like a flock of sheep, that I have but little left for the serious duties of my posi-tion."

These were familiar words, and when I went further down, and saw how much foremen's time and memories were taxed for means of attending at once and finally to their daily wants, I became con-vinced that the government methods, though bad enough, were not the only ones to be criticised.

In the matter of costs, too, I found great uncertainty : I found one business which had been exposed to expensive litigation, in-volving $6,000,000, to determine what was the true cost of ma-chinery sold by its agents at a commission based upon its cost of production. I found another entire trade based upon costs deter-mined, as one of its members writes me, by "thumb-sailing:" large establishments suffering from the competition of ignorant free lances, who in ruining themselves also injured their neighbors.

II.

The proposed system of shop accounts is based on two compen-sating principles.

1. The radiating from a central source, let us say the office, of all authority for expenditure of labor or material. These being, however they may be disguised, the elemental forms of all internal expenditure.

2. The converging toward the office from all circumferential points, of independent records of work done and expenses made by virtue of that authority.

Upon the free play of the forces thus defined there is but one essential restriction ; that every right to the means for executing an order shall be qualified by a responsibility, which shall be recorded in as great particularity of detail as the scheme of management adopted may require. This leads to a comparison of managements depending upon the automatic record of their results. The following discussion will show how easily and cheaply this end may be attained.

In a broad sense a manufactory may be considered as an engine for transforming material, and its efficiency, like the duty of a pump, may be measured by the ratio of the effort exerted to the effect produced.

It will not be disputed that this ratio is best expressed by the true costs of its products, and that managements may be compared by their costs.

The object of the proposed system of accounts is to provide automatic, and therefore impartial means for d termining the most probable cost of manufactures in gross, or in such detail as the expense of its determination may permit. This is no new necessity. It enters into the imminent questions of what we can afford to make at market prices; of what is the lowest selling price; and also into estimates relating to the differences caused by the addition or removal of parts and the substitution of processes.

The difficulty of analyzing the usual gross account of expenditures, the uncertainty of this analysis when made by clerks unfamiliar with the processes analyzed, and the evident objections to so employing the time of foremen, have generally led to more or less exact accurate estimates of cost by those whose management was more or less in question. I do not exclude the self-deception of absolute proprietors. These objections are increased as the product of an establishment is diversified, so that the more miscellaneous is the product, and hence the more necessary the knowledge of its difference in cost, the more difficult is this knowledge to obtain. A system which might serve a blast furnace would utterly fail in a repair shop, yet are not the accounts of repair shops often kept on blast-furnace principles?

It would seem that the practice of estimating costs would not be followed if a more positive method were available at a reasonable price.

The world has been working too long with existing methods for any one to hope to improve them; the change must be one of methods. I propose to replace the ordinary *ex post facto* analysis of expenses by a preliminary analysis of objects of expense to be followed by a synthesis of items of expense; made mechanically by sorting cards on which the objects of expense have been indicated at the time of expenditure, by the persons who most probably knew them best, in symbols significant to the least experienced compiler.

By thus defining every charge for labor and material, our accounts are, so to speak, balanced in advance, and it only remains to distinguish between specific and general expenses and properly to apportion the general expenses among the specific, in order to obtain the most probable cost of any specific object.

III.

A manufactory may be functionally divided into two main portions, the workshops and the office.

In the shops are performed the processes with the records of which the office is principally concerned; on one side stands the foreman expending labor in transforming material; on the other sits the clerk recording the results of the other's acts. Taking these two as typical figures, I propose:

1. To require the highest local authority to define the objects on which its resources are to be expended. In other words, what accounts are to be opened.

2. To require the foreman to define the object most probably benefiting by the expenditure which he directs, as nearly as possible at the time that the expenditure is made.

3. To require a clerk, independent of the foreman, to compile the record of the foreman's acts.

4. To provide a simple symbolic language, common to both office and workshop, by which the same object of expenditure, whether it be a product, a component or an operation of manufacture, shall always be called by the same name and by which the foreman's symbols shall suffice the clerk, without requiring of either a knowledge of the other's work.

5. To make each act of record an independent unit by entering it on a separate card, certified by significant punch-marks.

6. To save clerk's work in combining similar entries by assorting mechanically cards containing similar symbols, only transcribing the summation of the charges they contain.

7. To provide that no claim for labor shall be allowed, nor any material put in the way of expenditure unless charged to its most

probable object; so that to every right there shall attach a responsibility of record.

8. To provide for the transfer between general and specific expenses, of charges more probably belonging to either.

9. While allowing free play to the foreman, to increase correspondingly his responsibility as measured by—

1. The cost of specific work.

2. The ratio of his general expenses to the causes of such expenses.*

10. To eschew the use of books, except for final records, because of—

1. Their inflexibility; they can be used by but one person at a time.

2. The labor of combining similar entries made in them at different times and places.

3. The certainty that when used for memoranda, the effete matter will soon obscure the important, so that the longer an entry has escaped attention, the more certainly will it be neglected.

11. To prefer natural methods to arbitrary, so that those who may use the system shall of themselves tend to conserve it.

IV.

THE SHOP-ORDER SYSTEM.

The system has three principal objects in view :

1. The prompt performance of work by the prominence given to unfinished orders

2. The determination of the most probable cost of work and of management.

3. The keeping of an account of stock, in units of material as distinguished from their values.

It attains these objects by using three forms of cards, viz. :

1. Shop-order tickets, or warrants of expense, and records of expense reported on

2. Service cards.

3. Material cards.

---

* It will be seen that relieving himself under one head increases his responsibility under the other, so that the line of least resistance will be the truth. The same result is reached by requiring daily records, the immediate bearing of which on ultimate costs can hardly be appreciated at the time.

V.

Taking the above objects in the order of their importance we have—

1. Orders for work: shop-orders.

These are of two kinds, viz.:

1. Special orders, requiring the performance of specific work.

2. Standing orders, requiring the maintenance of certain facilities for the execution of the special orders.

These facilities may be either in charge of certain foremen, the costs of whose management we wish to compare, or may be too general in their nature to be assigned to any one department.

The first are called departmental, and the second, general, standing orders.

Designation:

The special orders are designated by serial numbers, beginning at 100, according to their sequence in the shop-order book.

Each department of the manufactory is known by a number, preferably in the order of work, and the standing order relating to its maintenance has the same number as the department. The numbers below 100 may be reserved for these orders; *e. g.*, 1. for the pattern-shop. 2. for the foundry, etc.

General standing orders may run from 50 to 100. In deciding how many and what they shall be, we must remember that our first analysis may safely be detailed because details may always be combined by neglecting their differences, and it is easier so to combine them than to analyze results too grossly stated into their component parts. The more complete is our preliminary analysis, the more stable will be our synthesis. The history of chemistry and of mathematics teaches this. In another sense we say " we divide that we may rule."

The following general standing orders are suggested:

51. Office expenses relating to factory.

52. Office expenses relating to sales.

53. Office, and other expenses which cannot be classified.

54. Power.

55. Heat.

56. Light.

57. Transportation, in and about factory.

58. Repairs of buildings, not departmental.

59. Superintendence, general.

For rent, insurance, taxes and the subdivision of general expenses, see Cost of Work, page 454.

Authority to issue orders.

The authority for all orders is vested in the office; but, as is customary, is more or less extended to include transactions between foremen. With the free exercise of this right is combined the incidental responsibility of a written record, retained by the recipient, who is in turn restrained by the automatic record of the cost of his work. Both records coming finally to the office, one foreman is accountable for the necessity of the order and the other for the cost of executing it. This principle of liberty qualified by responsibility runs throughout the plan.

Form of order.

The shop-order book provides a place for the record of every order originating in the office. A special order here receives its serial number, and work of a general nature worth special entry takes the number of its proper standing order.

To distribute orders, and for other purposes, the order ticket is devised. See duplicate form separated by a perforated line, page 447. A punch-mark of special design in the "authority" space, indicates the giver.

Standing orders and their numbers are circulated in lists which are soon memorized.

Course of tickets.

I shall describe the simplest case first, as its principles apply in all others.

1. For short jobs on which only one kind of work is done at a time, single tickets serve.

They are displayed in a rack in each foreman's office, while the work is in his shop. When the work is done he punches out his number* in the marginal line headed "completion" and passes the work and the ticket with it to the next foreman in order. This is continued until the ticket reaches the office, where the date of its completion may be entered in the shop-order book.

2. When work is to begin or continue in more than one depart-

---

* Men are known by the numbers of their shops or of the departments in which they work. In each department they are ranged by invariable numbers according to their importance, seniority, etc. Thus of shop, or department 3, the foreman is No. 301, the next man 302, and so on. This allows for 100 men in each department. If this number should be exceeded, many expedients of correction are possible. M.A. below signifies Master Armorer in arsenals; in private shops S. might be used for Superintendent.

ment at a time, separate tickets must be made out for each department. These issue directly from, and are returnable directly to,
the office, as soon as each department's work on the job is done.

Receipt.	M-A.	201.	205.	301.	401.	501.	601.	701.	801.
S-O.	; C.	; O.			; N.	;		188	

Authority,				Completed,				188	
Completion.	M-A.	201.	205.	301.	401.	501.	601.	701.	801.

Receipt.	M-A.	201.	205.	301.	401.	501.	601.	701.	801.
S-O.	; C.	; O.			; N.	;		188 .	

Authority,				Completed,				188	
Completion.	M-A.	201.	205.	301.	401.	501.	601.	701.	801.

3. Subordinate orders.

Foremen requiring the co-operation of others may originate tickets specifying the work to be done, by indicating the number of the

original order authorizing the work and punching the authority space with their special punches. The tickets are returned to the office by the recipient. They may well be white to distinguish them from office tickets, which may be of two or three different colors to indicate the relative urgency of the work they authorize.

Thus S-O. 789. *Build 6 double axle lathes,*

might be on a yellow ticket, indicating a staple manufacture, and—

S-O. 2, P. *Cut door, north side pattern-shop*

on a blue ticket, to indicate local work of an important nature. Such tickets emanating from the office would be in ink, and would refer to drawings, specifications, etc.; but a merely local order or foreman's request, such as

55, W, *Stop leak in steam coil,*

sent, say, by the master carpenter to the master machinist, might be in pencil on a white ticket.

It is desirable, but not essential, that subordinate orders be in writing. The advantage in definiteness, in responsibility, in the certainty of execution, and in the accuracy of the record which follow from writing them are so great as to outweigh the slight loss of time taken to fill them up and punch them. A package of tickets, a lead pencil and a ticket punch are all that a foreman needs for attending finally to any order which he is competent to give.

In complicated operations, where it is desirable to take heed of the receipt of orders on their delivery, duplicate tickets, such as shown in full, may be used to advantage. The duplicate ticket is also intended for a complete exhibit, say in the racks of the superintendent's office of unfinished work ordered by him or by his superiors. As the completed tickets come in from the foremen, he takes down his retained copy from the proper rack, punches it, and returns it to the main office, keeping that which he has received.

Advantages of order tickets.

Each foreman's unfinished work is always displayed before him, relieving his memory and permitting him to apply all his energy to active work. This applies in even greater measure to the superintendent.

For the orders in question the ticket represents both the work and the authority for doing it; and as no foreman receives work without its warrant, each one checks the other and prevents the loss or neglect of either. The loss of a ticket, at the worst, would correspond only to an order forgotten under common methods; in practice they are never lost.

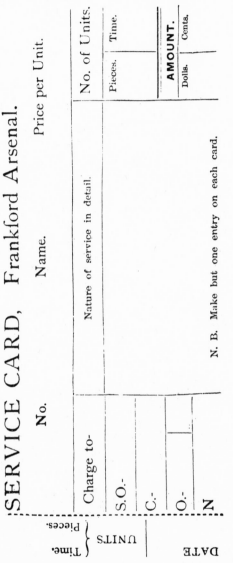

The tickets in the racks may be classified as work in hand or as not in hand, by departments, and in many other convenient ways. When returned to the office after completion, they may be re-

29

sorted according to objects worked on, forming an indefinitely expansible index to the order book.

VI.

RECORDS OF EXPENDITURE.

Having shown how an order, started from the heart of the administration or from one of its intermediate points, finds its way out to the circumference and along it ; and how, its work accomplished, it is by natural means brought back to its source, it remains to show how the records of the expense it has involved are similarly directed in their centripetal course.

The expenses of a workshop may be classified under two heads:

1. Services. $\begin{cases} \text{Internal.} \\ \text{External.} \end{cases}$
2. Material.

1. SERVICES.

Labor may be performed either within the establishment or without it. To both kinds of labor the name service is given, and their record is kept on uniform service cards. For internal services these are roughly bound into little books like check books, each page containing one card detachable like a bank check, and having a memorandum stub for the workman's private use. All cards are printed on one side of brown manilla paper.

Employment of service cards.

One of these cards, designed for arsenal use, and such as, with the addition of a space for "machine time," is used by one of our large locomotive factories, is reproduced full size on page 10.

R. G. & SON.		APR 2 1886	
No. 235.	Name. Lannigan,		Rate. 0.25.
ORDER NO.	PIECE.	WORK.	HOURS.
789	Spindles.	Planer.	10

The above is a full size cut of a similar card in simpler form, designed for day work in an establishment where no piece work is done. If greater simplicity were required, the two middle spaces might be omitted.

When a man is hired he receives a book in which, on each card his name and rate of wages are stamped. This certifies his employment to his foreman. He gets his book from his foreman in the morning and returns it at night with one page filled for every order on which he has worked during the day.

If he has worked all day on but one order, his writing may consist of its number and the number of time units in a working day. Thus, if the hour is taken as the time unit, he might write—

S-O. 789   Time units, 10

If time is kept by the half-hour it would read—

S-O. 789   Time units, 20   and so on.

The foreman looks over the books when handed in; if correct, stamps them with his dating stamp, tears out the leaves filled, and sends them to the office. The next morning he returns the books to the men.

The book serves a double purpose: it affords the workman an opportunity for making a definite charge for his labor, and it gives him the only opportunity of doing so. This makes certain a record of his employment during the time for which he is paid, and also affords original evidence from an impartial source as to the object on which that labor has been spent.

It takes the place of a roll call or time check. Early comers get their books at once and can go to work. Late comers are so marked on their own books. Those who leave early have their books verified at the time.

If a man has worked on several orders during the day he fills out a separate leaf for each order, the sum of the times equalling the total time, as before.

Piece work is similarly entered, the leaf being punched by the inspector. The time and piece records are independent of each other, so that if a batch of piece work should last a man for several days, he still makes his time record for those days at *no* price.

When the cards reach the office, daily, they are sorted, if need be, by names and the total time, pieces or wages entered in the time book. They are then re-sorted by orders and distributed in pigeon holes corresponding to the orders.

2. External services.

Outside services embrace freight, insurance, rent, taxes, telegraphing, attorney fees, etc., pertaining to factory. These cards, when approved, are filed like those first described.

Payment for such service must be similarly distributed among the shop orders benefiting by the expense. It is optional whether this shall be done for each bill before payment, or whether such charges shall be consolidated from the books monthly or oftener.

2. MATERIAL.

Material card.

This card, which is freely distributed in blank to the foremen, permits every transaction with material to be recorded. The accom-

```
                MATERIAL CARD.
                             APR 3 1886

    QUANTITY.              NAME.

ASSUMED.   UNIT.      N. B.   Make but one entry on each card.
   6       pcs.

ACTUAL.
  164      lbs.       Sanderson Steel 3/4 × 1 1/4

Price  Dolls.  Cts.      about 8 ft. long.
per
Unit.

     CHARGE TO      ||    CREDIT TO    ||   AMOUNT.
S-O.  C.  O.  N.  || S-O.  C.  O.  N.  || DOLLARS. | CENTS.
820   W            ||                  ||

   Ordered from Corning & Co.

REQUIRED   ●         CERTIFIED    ●
   BY                   BY
```

panying form is devised especially for private shops. If a foreman wants some steel he fills the card as shown, charging it to the order for which most probably needed. He makes a direct charge to a special order if possible; if not, then preferably to his departmental standing order. The foreman makes his entry in pencil, entries of price and amount being added by clerks.

Punching out "required by" he throws the card into his messenger box and concerns himself no more about it. Without awaiting a special time or opportunity for making known his wants; without awaiting the return from the office of his "requisition book," he has, at the very moment that the need of the steel presented itself, asked definitely and finally for what he wanted. He has set rolling a ball which will be in somebody's way until it is finally disposed of. At the office it may be approved or sent back for explanation, or simply suspended, without interfering with immediate action on other articles asked for at the same time. A long list is like a large bank-note, easy to carry, but hard to change.

Suppose that the requisition is approved by the superintendent's also punching "required by," the card is sorted with other cards of the same kind, say for hardware, the name of the dealer from whom the material is to be ordered attached, or not, at pleasure, and the card sent with others to the foreman or storekeeper who is to receive it on arrival. If to the foreman, he knows what to expect.

When the steel has come the quantity actually received is filled in, the receiver punches "certified by" or "received by," or whatever special form of acknowledgment may be required by the management, and sends the card to the bill clerk, who, after comparing it with the bill, and may be adding prices or amount, sends it to the cost clerk for filing in the proper pigeon-hole.

Let us suppose again that the foreman, having no immediate use for the steel, has charged his departmental standing order with it. By and by he finds that he wants 10 lbs. of it for a special job. He makes out another card, charging it to the special job and crediting himself accordingly on the same card and punches "certified by" as before. The converse is possible if he finds that he has charged too much to the special order first mentioned.

If he lets another foreman have steel he charges and credits appropriately between departmental orders, certifies the entry, and gets the other foreman to do so before he gives up the steel. The issuer keeps the punched card as his equivalent and sends it to the office for entry.

The card may also be used for reporting each batch of work packed or shipped or sent to the store-room or warehouse, as the custom of the place may require. Such cards contain a credit to the order under which the material has been made. They take theplace of all memoranda re-copied into lists for office use. Each card may start independently of the rest at the very time that the batch is done or inspected, so that there may be any number coming into the office during the day. Like the other cards they are movable memoranda, written once and for all by those responsible for their accuracy.

These are the simplest of many possible cases; I have so far been unable to imagine one in which the card fails to tell its story in the easiest and plainest way.

VII.

THE COST OF WORK.

This, second division of our subject, involves two elements:
1. The work done.
2. The cost of doing it.

The second of these divided by the first gives the price.

1. The work done.

An order having been completed, we may simply wish to know what it has produced.

This may be determined in any customary manner, subject to this precaution, that it is not always safe to assume that the exact number of articles ordered by the tickets has been made. The means described, page 14, are probably as easy and expeditious as any that can be devised.

The gross product is therefore easily determined, but, except in the crudest industries, this will hardly satisfy those in charge. There is scarcely any work which does not require some preparatory expense in the way of drawings, patterns, tools, etc., which may be useful for future work of the same kind.

We shall generally, therefore, require separate information as to—
1. What must be done again every time that such an order is repeated : what is made for sale.
2. What has been done in preparation, having, when the order is completed, a permanent value for future work of the same kind: what is made for the establishment.

In anticipation of such inquiries we provide in advance that all expenditures, besides being reported under the order authorizing them, shall be referred, under that order, either—
1. To "Work," symbol W., or
2. To "Plant," symbol P.

"Work" has been sufficiently defined above.

" Plant " includes drawings, patterns, machinery and special tools and fixtures not apt to be consumed during the execution of the order. Buildings, etc., are plant of standing orders, their extensive repairs and improvements are charged to P.; current repairs to W.

The simple analysis given suffices for miscellaneous products; but for the staple objects of manufacture for which a factory may be specially designed, such as guns, sewing, or other machines and appliances made on a large scale, we may also wish to be prepared to collect information relating to—

3. Their component parts.

4. The operations of manufacture through which these parts have passed.

These comprise all possible questions involving cost, which, to be truly answered, must be prepared for before the work to be analyzed is begun.

Therefore, although it is essential that only the number of the shop order appear on every record of expense, yet, for a full development of the system, it is desirable that every such record have room for four symbols, viz.:

S-O. The number of the *order* authorizing the expense.

C. The *character* (P. or W.) of the expense.

O. The component part or *object*, profiting by the expense.

N. The symbolic *number* of the mechanical operation performed on the object in question.

Room is therefore made for the symbols S-O.; C.; O.; and N. on the service and material cards already described. Only so many of these symbols need be used as the scheme of administration may require: some will be satisfied with gross costs, and will need only the first symbol; others will require plant to be separated from work; and others still, for staple manufactures, will want to know the cost of components and of the operations upon them. Such demands must be anticipated at a cost proportional to the benefit expected: as we would reap, so must we sow.

2. The cost of doing work.

The net cost consists of—

1. The specific expenses for labor.

2. The specific expenses for material.

These are also called the direct expenses, or those which can be charged directly to any particular job. Added to—

3. A proper proportion of the general annual, or indirect expenses, they make the gross cost.

It is comparatively easy to compute net costs by any of the usual methods. Their exactness depends upon the scale of trouble adopted, and, excepting errors of omission arising from unbalanced data, they may be assumed to be fairly accurate.

The main difficulty lies in apportioning those general or indirect expenses which cannot be referred to any special product. I therefore give special attention to this subject, as follows:

Apportioning the indirect expenses.

Factories are established for the profitable transformation of material by the organized employment of labor. How shall the indirect expenses be distributed? in ratio to the material or the labor? by quantity, or by value?

I believe that the incidental expenses are incurred for the purpose of making labor more effective, and that the more material enters as their divisor, the more does it vitiate the probability of the result.

For the more material costs, the more labor it has already had spent upon it; and the less, and not the more, does it need the facilities provided by the incidental expenses. On the other hand, the more men are employed, irrespective of their cost, the greater is the wear and tear, the waste, the cost for room light, heat and attendance, etc.

These and other similar considerations lead me to determine for each department a cost factor, as follows:

1. To distribute such general expenses as rent, insurance, taxes, etc., among departments profiting by them according to the most probable hypothesis.

2. To distribute last year's general standing orders or the unclassifiable current expenses among departments in proportion to the total day's work done in each department.

3. To add this amount for each department to the sum of its own expenses for the past year, as given by the cost of its departmental standing order.

4. To divide the gross amount thus obtained by the number of direct days' work done in each department during the past year, and so obtain a cost factor, say of $1.15 per day, by which the cost of every day's direct work in the present year must be increased in order to make it bear its most probable share of the cost of facilities provided for it.

Thus a man at $2.00 a day would be really costing $2.95, and a bill as follows:

15 days at $4.00		$60 00
6 " 2.50		15 00
27 " 1.25		33 75
48 days		$108 75

would be increased by $45.60, representing 48 days × cost factor of $0.95 per day.

The variation of the factor measures the foreman's management during the past year. Its amount is the cost of facilities for doing a day's work which is chargeable to a particular job.

VIII.

COMPUTATION OF COST.

Simple case: gross cost.

Our accounts may be on so simple a scale that we shall require no more than a simple statement of the gross cost of executing a given order. To obtain this we add up the charges contained on the service and material cards found in the pigeon-hole corresponding to the order in question. This gives the net cost. This, increased by the sum of the products obtained by multiplying the number of direct day's work done on the order in question in each department by the cost factor for that department, and diminished by the sum of the credits, gives the gross cost. In such a case the cards need only contain room for the symbol S-O.; the symbols C., O. and N. being omitted. I would recommend this simple method to beginners, although I believe that all will find it to their advantage as they become familiar with the system to analyze more closely. To such the following method commends itself.

Continued analysis of cost.

Sort the service and material cards belonging to a completed order according to Plant and Work, and add together their amounts under each head. Then correct the net cost so obtained for indirect expenses as already described.

The appraised value for future uses of plant should then be charged to the most probable standing order and credited to the cost of work. The amount thus determined when divided by the output gives the factory cost per piece, lb., etc. The factory cost increased by its proportion of the selling expenses, and profit added, gives the selling price.

For example: we find the total cost of S-O. 789 corrected for indirect expenses to be—

Plant..$ 50 00
Work.. 175 00
————
Gross cost........................$225 00

Suppose that by inspection of the cards we discover that no credit has been given for the contingent value of the patterns, which, let us say, is $25.00, and that they are kept in department No. 2. The omission of the foreman of No. 2, known as 201, should be supplied by making out a card as follows:

One set patterns.

CHARGE TO...2. CREDIT TO...789. AMOUNT, $25.00

This reduces the gross cost to $200.00, and increases correspondingly the liability of S-O. 2, subject to correction by inventory. (The annual inventory would correct the balance of 2, and hence affect distributively its charge for indirect expenses in future. This card should properly have been made out by 201 when the order was completed, thus clearing his mind of it, and leaving to higher authority only the task of revision.)

Detailed cost of components and of operations thereon.

If, as in staple products, the cost is needed in greater detail, we sort the cards by the object symbols, and those having like object symbols by the operation symbols, and service cards having like operation symbols by departments in which working, and those in each department by rates of wages. This being done, and the charges added together and labor increased by cost factor product, we may ascertain the most probable cost of every operation on every component. This is as far as any one would be apt to go.

Daily cost sheet.

By adding up daily the amounts in each pigeon-hole, and entering their net sum on the cost sheet, the office is kept informed how and where the money is going. The cards may then be sorted in continuous preparation for the analysis above described.

IX.

STOCK ACCOUNT.

By entering but one kind of material on each card we gain immensely in flexibility at a very small cost of trouble, for it takes but very little longer to fill, say three cards with one line each, than to write three lines on one card, and when written the cards are independent of one another. (This applies to both service and material cards.)

This feature is particularly valuable in the accountability for Government property, which happens to be altogether by items, without regard to values. An instance of its immediate utility to private works will suffice. After the sortings, previously described, the material cards in each pigeon-hole may be re-sorted by the names of material upon them; this forms a convenient bill of material, the difference between which and even careful estimates will often prove surprising.

Space fails me to describe all the advantages following the independence of these units of record, which, like that of the printer's type, adapts them to an immense variety of uses. I have tried them in every supposable case of the affairs of an arsenal, trammeled by all the precautions imposed by a most jealous audit, and have yet to find a case in which they fail.

X.

APPLICATION.

The data for an illustrative case are derived from the analysis of the expenses of a hypothetical stove foundry which for the past two years has been the subject of discussion by the National Association of Stove Manufacturers.*

It had been estimated by one of the most experienced members of that association that the gross annual expenses of a foundry capable of turning out about 3,000 tons of a fair assortment of stoves per annum were about $321,000, divided as follows:

LABOR.

	Per ton.	Per 3,000 tons.
Moulding	$24 00	$72,000 00
Mounting	8 00	24,000 00
Pattern making	1 45	4,350 00
Pattern fitting and repairs	1 50	4,500 00
Pattern moulding	25	750 00
Carpenters	1 25	3,750 00
Cupola-men, breaking iron, etc	75	2,250 00
Cleaning and piling	2 00	6,000 00
Engineer	30	900 00
Shipping	1 00	3,000 00
General labor	2 00	6,000 00

* It is fully analyzed in the *New York Metal Worker*, February 6, and in the *Chicago Artisan* of February 6 and 13, 1886.

LABOR—*continued.*

	Per ton.	Per 3,000 tons.
Watchman .... $	25	$750 00
Foreman, moulding and melting.	50	1,500 00
Clerks	50	1,500 00
Trucking.....................................	75	2,250 00
Miscellaneous and pilferings	50	1,500 00
	$45 00	$135,000 00

MATERIAL.

Foundry Costs.	Per ton.	Per 3,000 tons.
Iron..... .... $20 00		$60,000 00
Mounting materials, not including nickel panels and rails, etc...............................	8 00	24,000 00
Fuel for all purposes...........................	2 75	8,250 00
Moulding sand and clay.........................	40	1,200 00
Facing	25	750 00
Patterns, flasks and lumber material	75	2.250 00
Shipping material.............................	10	300 00
Freight and expressage...........................	1 25	3,750 00
Machinery and tools............................	1 75	5,250 00
Repairs	40	1,200 00
Gas and oil....................................	20	600 00
Stationery and books...........................	10	300 00
Rent....	1 00	3,000 00
Insurance	40	1,200 00
Taxes....................................... ..	25	750 00
Miscellaneous and pilferings..............	40	1,200 00
Castings broken and discarded that have been paid for...	1 00	3,000 00
	$39 00	$117,000 00

SELLING EXPENSES.

	Per ton.	Per 3,000 tons.
Allowances of various kinds..... .. ..$1 25		$3,750 00
Attorneys' fees	25	750 00
Advertising, catalogues, etc......................	1 75	5,250 00
Bad debts....................................	2 00	6,000 00
Clerks..	1 60	4,800 00
Freight on stoves delivered......................	1 00	3,000 00
Gas and oil.......	10	300 00
Insurance	20	600 00
Interest.......................................	2 00	6,000 00
Discount for cash	2 50	7,500 00
Miscellaneous and pilferings......................	50	1,500 00
Postage, express and telegrams	1 00	3,000 00
Rent...	1 00	3,000 00
Stationery......................................	15	450 00
Traveler's wages................................	2 75	8,250 00

SELLING EXPENSES—*continued*.

	Per ton.	Per 3,000 tons.
Travelers' expenses and general traveling..........	3 25	9,750 00
Taxes..	20	600 00
President and Secretary	1 50	4,500 00
	$23 00	$69,000 00

RECAPITULATION.

Total labor cost...	$135,000 00
Total foundry cost material...............................	117,000 00
Total selling expense......................................	69,000 00
	$321,000 00

It must now appear that the essence of the system proposed is to afford means of making definite charges of expense in the following order of preference:

1. Special order, as plant or work.
2. Departmental standing order.
3. General standing order.

For the foundry let us call our departments and their standing orders as follows:

1. Pattern shop.
2. Moulding.
3. Melting.
4. Mounting.
5. Foundry, unclassified.

These comprise the manufactory proper. Now, let all the other departments be consolidated under one head,

10. The selling department.

The number of departments is limited for simplicity's sake. The more they are divided the more exact will be the resulting costs; but the more trouble will it take to keep the accounts separate.

Each of the items of expense named (pages 459–461) was distributed among the departments named, and for each item of labor the number of day's work corresponding to the amount distributed, at an assumed average rate of wages, was also stated.

Labor, which, like moulding, mounting, pattern and flask-making, is susceptible of being charged to special orders, was called direct work, and separated from that like engineers, cupola-men, and superintendence belonging to the standing orders, and a result obtained which represented, most probably, the actual results of one year's work under the system proposed.

TABLE NO. I

ANALYSIS OF LABOR CHARGES.

DEPARTMENT.	DIRECT. Chargeable to Special Shop Orders.		INDIRECT. Chargeable to Departmental or General Shop Orders. Standing.	
	Value.	No. of Days' Work.	Value.	No. of Days' Work.
1. Patterns	$10,500	4,500	$1,350	600
2. Moulding	72,000	24,000	8,000	6,980
3. Melting	....	....	4,050	2,270
4. Mounting	24,000	14,000	1,450	925
5. Foundry in general	....	...	6,400	3,615
Totals	$106,500	42,500	$21,250	14,390

Labor.   Value.   Days' Work.
Direct $106,500 42,500
Indirect 21,250 14,390

$127,750   56,890

TABLE NO. II.

ANALYSIS OF CHARGES FOR MATERIAL.

DEPARTMENTS.	Direct.	Indirect.
1. Patterns	$1,500	$583
2. Moulding	....	4.863
3. Melting	....	72,483
4. Mounting	20,000	5,681
5. Foundry in general	....	12,915
Totals	$21,500	$96,345

Combining Tables I. and II., we find the following total indirect charges :

TABLE NO. III.

TOTAL INDIRECT CHARGES PER ANNUM PER DEPARTMENT.

DEPARTMENTS.	Labor.	Material.	Total.
1. Pattern..................	$1,350	$483	$1,833
1. Moulding	8,000	4,863	12,863
3. Melting.................	4,050	72,403	76,453
4. Mounting...............	1,450	5,681	7,131
5. Foundry in general.......	6,400	12,915	19,315
Totals.................	$21,250	$96,345	$117,595

Expenses for shipping (labor and material), warehousemen, cartage, watchman, freight, and pilfering transferred from the foundry data, increased the sales' account to $75,405 which is about 30 per cent. of the balance of $245,595 devoted to manufacturing.

For the present we set aside the direct expenses and seek how best to apportion the indirect expenses among them. This we do by distributing the most general charges among those less so, until the cost factor for each department is obtained, as follows:

We first take the total general foundry expenses, $19,315, and divide them among 1, 2, 3, 4, according to the *total* days' work done in each department, as follows:

TABLE IV.

DISTRIBUTION OF GENERAL FOUNDRY EXPENSES AMONG DEPARTMENTS.

DEPARTMENTS.	Days' Work per Annum. From Table I.			Share per total d. w. of $19,315 in Table III.	Total Indirect Charges per Department, from Table III.	Gross total, Indirect, per Department.
	Direct.	Indirect.	Total.			
	d. w.	d. w.	d. w.	$	$	$
1. Patterns........	4,500	600	5,100	1,850	1,833	3,683
2. Moulding.................	24,000	6,980	30,980	11,230	12,863	24,093
3. Melting...........		2,270	2,270	823	76,453	77,276
4. Mounting.	14,000	925	14,925	5.412	7,131	12,543
Totals	42.500	10,775	53,275	19,315	98,280	117,595

Next, except for Melting, which will be treated later, we divide the gross total indirect expenses for each department by the number of days' *direct* work done in it during the past year, and get the Cost Factors per department as follows: *

1. Patterns...$0 82
2. Moulding 1 00
4. Mounting.. 0 90

It is supposed that under the same management the cost factors will not vary greatly from year to year. In this respect they will resemble to some extent the phenomena of life insurance; so that such variations as may be found may be attributed to causes the effects of which in future cases may be closely approached. But in gaining this experience the following discussion may serve.

The indirect expenses may be divided into two classes: those like rent, insurance, salaries, etc., which are fixed charges; and those which, like attendance, wear and waste, have a closer relation, say a direct ratio, to the number of men employed.

Calling the fixed charges for a given time F; the variable charges, V; the number of direct days' work in the same time, D; and the cost factor, either for the whole factory or for any one department, C, we have

$$C = \frac{F + V}{D}$$

If we change suddenly the number of men employed, then D will become D'; and V will become V', and

$$C' = \frac{F + V'}{D'}$$

For example, if $F = \$12,000$; $V = \$28,319$, and $D = 42,500$ d. w.

Then $C = \$0.95$.

If we double the number of men employed, on direct work only, then

$$C' = \pm \$0.80.$$

If we discharge half the force,

$$C_1 = \pm \$1.23, \text{etc.}$$

---

* We may simply take the quotient of the aggregate indirect expenses of the three departments by their aggregate of days' direct work (\$0.95) as a gross cost factor for them all. This course will be more simple than the other, but its simplicity will be purchased at too great a cost if we lose the opportunity for keeping the foremen up to the mark by comparing the expenses of their respective managements.

In the Melting Department, as the cost of iron in good castings depends so much more upon the output than upon the number of men employed, I disregard the men and divide the cost by the weight of good castings produced, say 6,000,000 lbs.; this gives a cost per lb. (not for melted iron, as it is often called, but for good castings) of 1.288 cents per lb.; and this is taken as the cost factor of that department.

COST OF A STOVE.

Now, suppose that we have finished an order calling for 500 stoves of a special size and pattern, and that from overrunning or by direction 521 happen to be made with a lot of spare parts estimated to be worth, say, $200. Also suppose that the patterns are estimated to be worth half cost for future work. We may establish the cost per department as follows :

1. Patterns.

These have all been made by day labor, charged to the order from day to day. So has the material. We find that they have cost as follows :

```
Labor, direct, at average of $2.75 ..........................$1,500 00
Cost of facilities, 545 days' work at 82 cents.................   447 00
Value of material, estimated..............................   513 00
                                                          ----------
    Cost of patterns.......................................$2,460 00
```

2. Moulding.

If this is done by the day and an account be kept, as with the patterns, the same course is followed, except that no special charge is made for materials, all of which comes out of the cost factor. But since in stove foundries, moulders work almost altogether by the piece, and owing to the great number of different parts of different stoves which they are apt to mould at the same time, it is almost impossible for them to keep their time on each order ; the time may be approximated by dividing the total piece price per stove by the nearest average daily earnings. Thus, if the sum of the piece prices on the stove in question be $2.25, and the average earnings per day of moulders employed on this class of work be $3, each stove will take on the average three-fourths of a day's work to mould, and the cost of moulding may be expressed as follows :

```
Piece price......................................................$2 25
Cost of facilities, viz.: 0.75 day's work at $1 per day............   75
                                                          ----------
    Cost of moulding each .....................................$3 00
521 stoves at $3.00 .........................................$1,563 00
```
30

3. Melting.

Suppose that the stoves weigh 347 pounds each; $347 \times 521 \times 1.288$ cents...$2,328 00

4. Mounting.

Either of the plans described for the pattern shop or moulding floor may be followed according to circumstances; but a third case may present itself, where the mounting is done by a contractor who employs a number of men, the establishment furnishing power, tools and room, and paying the contractor by the piece. This presents special difficulties, for while we pay the contractor by the piece, he probably pays his men by the day, and makes no attempt to distribute their time, contenting himself with securing a profit on their aggregate wages.

In such a case two methods are possible. The first and most accurate requires knowledge of the average profit made by the contractor and of the average number of men he employs per day. Then the men's share of the piece price paid for mounting any stove, divided by their average daily wages, is equal to the number of days' work in mounting that stove.

For example: suppose that owing to ignorance on both sides of the actual amount of labor required to mount any particular stove, and to the concessions which in long business intercourse of this kind supply the place of competition, the prices paid the contractor are so fixed as to allow him in the long run a profit of about ten per cent. on his expenses for labor.

This will give the men about 90 per cent. of the piece price, which, when divided among them, gives, say, an average per man of $1.50 per day. Supposing the firm pays for mounting our stove $1.25; then it takes

$$\frac{90}{1.50} \text{ of } \$1.25 = 0.75 \text{ day's work to mount that stove.}^*$$

The contractor's estimated profit should be charged to the general expense of mounting (S. O., No. 4), as he is virtually a foreman under a specially strong incentive to make his men work. It may seem rather inquisitorial to require the contractor to expose his pay roll; but this is justified by the circumstance that the

---

* (Proof.   The contractor gets $521 \times \$1.25 =$....................$651 25
  Of which the men get 90 per cent., or................. 586 12
  Which, at $1.50 per day $= 390.75$ days' work,
  Or for 521 stoves................. 0.75 day's work per stove.)

foundry furnishes the facilities which are occupied, worn and wasted more nearly in proportion to the number of men employed than to any other quantity.

Now, suppose the contractor keeps his profits to himself. We merge him with the men, and knowing, for police purposes if for no others, how many men are employed per day in a given time, the quotient of the contractor's gross receipts for that time, divided by the number of days' work done in his department during that time, gives the average cost of a day's work, which, divided into the piece price per stove, gives the day's work on that stove for mounting.

We can now sum up the cost of mounting per stove as follows:

Contract price..	$1 25
$0.75 day's work × $0.90 (cost factor, p. 25)...................	0 67
Material, per material cards, or estimated from list of material as shown by drawings...................................	1 10
Total per stove..	$3 02
Total for 521 stoves..	$1,574 00

Omitting ornaments, nickel work, tiles, crating, etc., all of which can be charged directly, we may sum up as follows:

COST OF SHOP-ORDER, No. 7,654, FOR 521 "O. K." STOVES.

Patterns..		$2,460 00
Moulding...		1,563 00
Melting (iron in castings)....................................		2,328 00
Mounting...		1,574 00
Gross cost...		$7,925 00
Deduct ½ patterns................................	$1,230 00	
Extra parts......................	200 00	$1,430 00
521 stoves at $12.46..		$6,495 00
Foundry cost, each...		$12 46
Selling expenses, at 30 per cent.............................		3 74
Net cost...		$16 20
Profit, say at 10 per cent....................................		1 62
Selling price..		$17 82

Let us suppose that another set of men are employed, who work so much faster that we can afford to increase their wages 50 per cent., the direct outlay for labor remaining unaltered.

The time on the job, and consequently its share of the indirect

expenses, will be $\frac{1}{3}$ less than before, and, the cost factor determined with correspondingly slow labor remaining unaltered, we
shall save $395.00 in the cost of the stoves, or about 6 per cent.*

Of course, if we continue with this grade of labor for the same
yearly product, our cost factor may increase; but this tendency
will probably be diminished either by an increase in product for
the total number of days' work per annum, or by a diminution in
interest charges on invested and working capital, or by both causes
and other causes also.

The example is offered to show in dollars and cents that cheap
labor is not always profitable; and how the rate of work enters
into the rate of wages.

It will be observed that as soon as the patterns are made and
the piece prices for moulding and mounting established, the selling
price of the stove may be known almost as well before it is made,
as afterward. The advantage of this is apparent.

In a foundry such as has been described, the use of the service
cards might be confined to pattern makers, and to a few other employees whose time is distributed among special orders.

General labor constantly engaged on standing orders might be
cared for by the usual methods of time keeping, and piece workers by the means described.

Charges for material purchased might be made in bulk, on the
principles set forth, from the bills received from dealers, and trans-
fers of charges by foremen be also by values in bulk. Or charges
for material entering into the cost factor might be made annually
as shown by item (e) in the following statement:

	Dr.	Cr.
On hand per last inventory.......................... a		..
Procured since last inventory........................ b		..
On hand per present inventory............................... c		
Accounted for by direct charges to fabrications since last inventory, made out from drawings or specifications, p. 28... d		
Balance charged to proper departmental standing order.......... e		

Experience only could tell how much detail it would pay to
neglect.

---

* The saving will depend somewhat upon the departments in which an increase of earnings is allowed. The illustration supposes the increase to be
uniform.

Mr. W. E. Partridge.—I wish to direct attention to a point in Mr. Towne's paper which is usually overlooked by manufacturers. He says that in the establishment he mentions, the cost of labor has in certain instances been greatly reduced, while the earnings of the men have not been encroached upon. This is a vital point. The almost universal tendency of manufacturers is toward a reduction of wages as an easy and obvious method of reducing the cost of production. In this, as in most mechanical work, the easy and obvious method is the wrong one. Both manufacturer and workman have a common commercial interest in seeing the earnings of the employee very large.

It has been a notorious fact that in certain lines of manufactures, goods were most cheaply produced in that portion of New England where wages were highest, and were most expensive to make in certain parts of the West where wages were but one-third as large.

How to cut down the price of piecework is usually considered a problem for the manufacturer only, and one which, when solved, can only result in a reduction of earnings. This is by no means necessary. The employee may be as steadily and earnestly considering the methods for reducing the prices of piecework as the proprietor of the establishment himself. In an extensive manufactory, under the superintendence of one of our members, I believe, a system is in use which is worthy of consideration by all manufacturers and engineers. A large proportion of the men are on piecework. When one of the men devises any method or new machinery by which the time required to perform any operation can be shortened, the works at once proceed to establish a new price or schedule for that class of work, and the men receive one-half of the gain thus made. If the improved method, machine, or tool originates in the drawing-room or office the men get one-third and the establishment two-thirds of the saving. When the improved methods call for new tools, dies, "jigs," etc., they are made at the expense of the works in all cases.

Under such a system every man is as busily employed with the problem of reducing the price of piecework and the cost of production to his superintendent or employer. In this establishment it is no uncommon thing to have an application from a workman for a new and reduced price to be set on some kind of piecework, the application being based on improved tools or methods of his own invention.

When the work of erection is done by gangs of men, the same rules are enforced. If a job is completed in less than the standard time, the overplus is paid for as overtime. When a new adjustment of work is made, the gangs get their share of the advantage. The practical application of this plan makes every man an interested overseer, and sets before him a premium for the improvement of every part of every process or operation, while it drives even the day laborer with the same spur to make every day's work as large as possible. In this way every man becomes a most efficient co-laborer with the manufacturer.

Very material advantages accrue from the employment of high-priced workmen. Large earnings employ valuable men with large producing powers. They become property owners. They are conservative and respectable members of society, and invariably throw their influence on the side of law and order. Such men can feel an intelligent interest in the success of the establishment. Under a system like that just outlined the loafer is either driven to work or fired out of the shop. Every man becomes an overseer with powers to act, which he does not fail to exercise, and he does not omit to keep up both standards of quality and quantity. He is a most vitally interested party, becoming virtually a silent partner upon whose co-operation implicit confidence may be placed.

The question is sometimes asked in this connection, How shall we keep up the standard of work as regards quality? Where machines are built, after the usual inspection is provided for, it is sufficient to guarantee the quality to the customer, and then make the erecting gang responsible for all defects in quality which they could have detected while erecting. A discoverable error in workmanship, or flaw in material, is charged to those who put the machine together. When those who erect find flaws or poor work, the last man who expended labor on the piece, and who had an opportunity to detect the trouble, sustains the loss. Every man who passes work forward becomes responsible for its quality to the man who next handles the work. This, at first sight, may appear a little unjust, but it is not so. A man, even in the inspection-room, may feel disinclined to turn a piece of poor work back upon some man with whom he is on friendly terms, but if he knows that the penalty will fall on his own shoulders, or rather his own pocket, he will not hesitate. Self-interest soon adjusts the whole matter.

Men refuse to accept poor stock to work on. Poorly finished or imperfect work is turned back at every step. Poor workmen are weeded out, and the quality once established is always kept up.

Mr. Chas. H. Fitch.—I would like to touch upon the question which is brought up in Mr. Towne's phrase, "without encroaching upon the earnings of the men engaged." It is beyond question that the ever narrowing tendency to consider and achieve wealth alone is a curse rather than a blessing. It is as truly economy to elevate the standard of manhood as it is to elevate proficiency in money-making, and it comes as near mechanical engineering. An economic section of this Society ought to consider the condition of mechanic labor and the means by which it may enjoy a more gratifying compensation. The manufacturer, however philanthrophic his disposition, is himself in the hands of iron-bound circumstances, and is often unable to do what he would in this direction. The economic section can, however, secure some concert of action and be the means of making it a matter of wholesome emulation to establish superior conditions for the performance of labor. I think that the author of the paper will certainly concur in this, that it would be laudable to set the mark a little higher than the mere avoidance of encroachment upon the earnings of the men engaged.

Mr. Jno. W. Anderson.—Mr. Metcalfe has placed the manufacturers of this country under obligations to him by the prominence which he is giving to the question of shop accounts. I can vouch for the value of the system, as I have used it with slight difference in form. While perhaps in most shops cards or order-slips would be just the thing, there are some kinds of manufacturing where, I think, books are preferable to cards for entering shop orders; that is, orders given to the several departments for work to be done. A little of my experience in this line may be useful in showing modifications of the system. About seven years ago I took charge of a large manufacturing establishment which embraced twelve different departments, each having a foreman. The plan of giving orders then in use was to write the order on a sheet with printed heading and send it to the foreman of the first department interested in the job. When he had finished his part of the work he handed it to the next foreman, and so on until the job was completed.

I soon found that in that factory there were objections to that plan. The sheets, or slips, would usually get soiled and torn, and frequently literally worn out before reaching their destination. Sometimes they would get lost. There was no record left in the departments of the work done. With most of the orders it was necessary that the work should be in progress in several different departments at the same time. If the foremen depended on one slip, it was inconvenient and troublesome for them. If several slips were issued, it complicated the checking and filing them in the office.

After giving the matter some thought, I adopted a set of order-books to take the place of the order-slips. The books adopted were plain ruled records, with a wide margin on one side of the page. The departments were numbered from one upward.

The book containing the original orders is kept in the superintendent's office, and each department is supplied with a similar book, except in size. Each order is numbered, and the same number is u ed throughout the works. When an order is entered on the superintendent's book, he looks it over and marks on the margin the numbers of the departments that will take part in the work, as shown in Form 1.

FORM 1.

	No.
1.	
2.	
3.	
4.	
5.	

The messenger brings the department books to the office when instructed to do so, and the superintendent or his clerk enters the orders on them and returns them to the foremen.

When the foreman of a department finishes his part of an order he checks it off by recording the date on the margin. At the same time he reports it to the superintendent by signing and dating a blank like Form 2, and drops it into his letter-box.

FORM 2.

S. Manufg. Co.

........:....................188

Superintendent of Construction.

 Sir: Order No......was completed in my department to-day.

    ....*Foreman.*

These reports, with other communications from the foremen, are collected by the messenger twice each day and delivered to the superintendent's office. The superintendent checks off the orders on his book as shown in Form 3.

FORM 3.

	No. 524.
2/8/84. 1.	
2.	
3.	
4.	
5.	

For example, foreman of department No. 1 reports order No. 524 completed in his department on February 8, 1884.

The superintendent turns to that order on his book and enters the date on the line numbered 1 on the margin.

At the same time he fills out a blank, like Form 4, and drops it into the letter-box, to be delivered by the messenger to the foreman who takes the job next.

FORM 4.

S. Manufg. Co.

Superintendent's Office,

.........................188

Foreman, Dept. No....

Sir: Order No....is ready for your Dept.

.......................*Supt.*

Form 4 has two or three blank lines for any special instructions the superintendent may desire to give, as for example: Commence work on this order at once. Or, Give this order preference over all others, etc.

When the superintendent has checked his book in this manner from the reports of the foremen, he can see at a glance the progress each order has made, and each step toward completion has its date recorded.   Should the superintendent find that an order is delayed in any department he fills out blank, Form 5, to which the foreman is bound to reply at once.

FORM 5.

S. Manufg. Co.

Superintendent's Office,

.......................188

Foreman, Dept. No....

Sir: I have no report from your dept. on order No....

Please report progress.

.......................*Supt.*

By this system the time required by the superintendent to watch the progress of the work need not exceed one hour each day, even when there are a large number of orders going through the factory at one time, thus leaving a large amount of time for legitimate duties, which in some shops is spent in "shooing" the orders through. Every foreman has a record of what he has done. If it is necessary or desirable for him to refer to a past order he has it before him. If anything is forgotten or mistake made the record is there to show for itself, and it is easy to fix it upon the right person.

As soon as an order is given each foreman knows his duty in the case, and he is enabled to provide for it in advance if necessary.

The system has worked so satisfactorily in the factory referred to that there has been no desire to change it.

Mr. F. W. Taylor.—I have read with very great interest Mr. Metcalfe's paper, as we at the Midvale Steel Co. have had the experience, during the past ten years, of organizing a system very similar to that of Mr. Metcalfe. The chief idea in our system, as in his, is, that the authority for doing all kinds of work should proceed from one central office to the various departments, and that there proper records should be kept of the work and reports made daily to the central office, so that the superintending department should be kept thoroughly informed as to what is taking place throughout the works, and at the same time no work could be done in the works without proper authority. The details of the system have been very largely modified as time went on, and a consecutive plan, such as Mr. Metcalfe proposed, would have been of great assistance to us in carrying out our system. There are certain points, however, in Mr. Metcalfe's plan, which I think our experience shows to be somewhat objectionable. He issues to each of the men a book, something like a check-book, containing sheets which they tear out, and return to the office after stating on them the work which they have done. We have found that any record which passes through the average workman's hands, and which he holds for any length of time, is apt either to be soiled or torn. We have, therefore, adopted the system of having our orders sent from the central office to the small offices in the various departments of the works, in each of which there is a clerk who takes charge of all orders received from, and records returned to, the central office, as well as of all records kept in the department.

The clerk or clerks in these department offices write, in all cases where it is practicable, under the direction of the foreman of the department, written orders stating what work is to be done, and how it is to be done; what order number to charge it to, and what drawings and tools are to be used, etc.

These orders are locked up in suitable bulletin-boards with glass doors in front, so that the men can see but not handle them. Each man in the shop receives from the shop clerk a note or a card for every job that he is to undertake, which refers him to the more elaborate order locked into the bulletin-board. The note which each workman receives gives him the proper authority for doing his work, and at the same time insures the concern to a certain extent against spoiled work, which so frequently results from misunderstanding verbal directions. These notes are also the means of conveying all desired information about the work to which they refer, both from the foreman and from the man who is doing the work, for keeping the records in the small offices as well as in the main office. We find that there are a great many records which it is desirable to keep close to the department in which the work is going on, for which there is comparatively little need in the central office.

For instance, it may be very desirable for each foreman to be able to place his hands at a few minutes' notice on the record of the piece of work last done, similar to that which he is about to do. For those records, of course, he could not afford the delay of sending to the main office, and it would be a very difficult matter, if they were kept there, for him to obtain the information which he desired without going himself and saying just what he wanted. If he, however, has a series of card records kept in his own office, close to where he works, and if those records are arranged, not chronologically, but on loose cards, which can be filed in such a way that the record of each job as it is finished will be placed next to that of the job which most nearly resembles it. If the records are kept on cards instead of books, the foreman can with great ease obtain any information about former jobs similar to the one he is about to start on, either in the way of mistakes made, or suggestions as to the best method of accomplishing the work, the cost, the time, or the man who did the work, etc. In our system only such information is sent to the central office as is there needed to keep them posted as to the cost and progress of the work and the men's time. While in the department office is kept much fuller information about the work, in fact everything which the foreman may find it useful to know.

Mr. W. F. Durfee.—I think this subject is one of the most important that has ever been brought to the notice of this Society, and while I fully concur in the opinion of Mr. Towne, that it is in the highest degree deserving of our consideration, I am somewhat in

doubt as to the advisability of organizing a separate section for that
purpose, being fully persuaded that every engineer here who is interested in the management of works, or ever expects to be, will be
a member of that section, and we should simply resolve ourselves
into a " committee of the whole " to consider that subject.   I think
it is perfectly proper to bring it before the
Society as a body, and that this discussion
will demonstrate that it will have an interest for all of us.

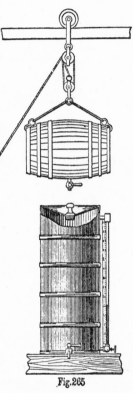

As an illustration of the importance of
this subject, I will state some facts in my
own experience.   Some years ago, I was
called to the supervision of a very large
works, employing at times a thousand
men, and I found an utter destitution of
all system for determining the cost of
work done.   As an illustration of the state
of the accounts, I would state that in the
assets of the company and on its books
there appeared a credit of six thousand
tons of a certain kind of coal.   As a matter of fact, there was no such coal on the
premises.   The coal at that time was worth
six dollars a ton on the ground, and there
was an asset that it would puzzle a book-
keeper to account for.   There was no system whatever for distributing stores at the
works, and no proper store-room account.
One of the important items of supply was
oil.   The method of distributing that oil
consisted in turning the barrels into an oil

Fig.265

room in the charge of a man, and everybody who wanted oil came
there and got it without reference to where it was to be used.
There was no method of telling whether they carried it home, or
into one department of the mill or another, or did anything with it.

This state of affairs was of course intolerable, and therefore in
order to effect a radical change and to keep an accurate account of
the receipt and consumption of oil, I had six cans made, each of
which would hold a little more than two barrels.   The illustration
(Fig. 265) gives a good idea of the construction of one of the cans,
the upper end being shown in section.

The upper head of each can was made in the form of an inverted cone, having a screw plug at its apex. On the right-hand side of each can was a glass gauge-tube whose scale was graduated by pouring oil into the can one gallon at a time, and marking on the scale its level in the gauge-tube, thus eliminating the effect of all errors of form or size from the scale. This work was done by the official sealer of weights and measures of the locality, and when complete he placed his official seal upon each can.

Over the range of six cans there was an over-head railway so located that a barrel of oil could be hoisted and run into either of the cans. Thus the store-keeper had a means of checking the receipts of oil. Previous to the adoption of this arrangement the oil was always paid for as per invoice. No one knew whether the barrels were full or half full, and soon after the construction of the measuring cans, their use detected a shortage of about 25 per cent. of the oil that was charged. We soon straightened that up, and though we continued to purchase of the same parties, their invoices always agreed with our receipts of oil as measured in these cans, and we had no further trouble with shortage. For distributing the oil to the several departments of the works I adopted the following system : I had a number of cards printed of different colors, each color designating a different department of the works. On these different colored cards were printed the words " One gallon," " A quart," or "A pint" of oil; a blank giving space to specify in pencil the quality of the oil wanted. The store-keeper kept an account with each department, and distributed at the beginning of the month a certain number of these tickets to the superintendent of each department of the works, and when there was any oil wanted in a department, its superintendent would send a man to buy it of the store-keeper with one of those tickets. As the oil was sold, the tickets received for it were deposited in a locked tin box, and on the first of every month this box was opened, the tickets assorted, and the value represented by each color charged up to its proper department.

One month's trial of the above described system demonstrated a saving sufficient (in the matter of oil alone) to pay all the clerical force necessary to the carrying out of a complete system of cost accounts for the whole works. One of the principal features of the system of cost accounts was this, viz.: All supplies which were consumed in the establishment were when purchased charged to store-room account, and the store-keeper kept an account with each department of the works as rigidly as if he were a private merchant dealing with the same department. In this way waste, and what was far worse, petty thievery, was prevented and a degree of responsibility fixed upon the heads of the several departments which resulted in increased efficiency to a marked degree.

Mr. Oberlin Smith.—In giving a little discussion to the first two papers, I want to say that, like Mr. Durfee, I have some doubts about the establishment of a separate section in this Society for the consideration of economic subjects. I heartily believe in considering these things, and I suppose after awhile our Society will be so large that we may want to divide into sections as does the "British Association" and the "American Association," but whether the time has yet come to split into two as a preliminary thing to splitting into three, or four, or five eventually, I don't know; perhaps it has. If we do not do that, I hope that this subject will be agitated at future meetings—that papers will come in, and that the whole thing will be thoroughly discussed, for it needs discussion very badly indeed. The waste in ordinary shops, especially in small machine-shops throughout the country, is very great, and more than a casual observer would be apt to suspect. One thing that needs looking up a great deal more is shop organization—the officers of the shop and their relations to each other. Now, in cotton-mills there is a regular organization, just as much as there is in the army. Everybody knows his duty and his responsibility, and to whom he is responsible and what for. But in machine-shops there is no regular definite system. In some cases the foreman is the head officer outside of the office, and the gang bosses come next under him. In some cases there is a superintendent and several foremen under him. In some cases gang bosses are absent entirely. The comparison of experience in these matters, and a careful thinking out of the best organization, will no doubt result in a great deal of saving of money to the country. Whatever the Society shall decide to do about another section, they will be working in the right direction in taking cognizance of this subject.

In regard to Captain Metcalfe's paper, I am inclined to think from what I have studied of his very valuable book and of the paper, that his system is an excellent one. Of course, it needs modification to suit particular cases. There is some question in my mind whether or not the plan of using a separate ticket for every little transaction is always the best. I have no doubt that it is, in cases where each man does a good deal of one kind of work. But in a machine-shop where there is a production of a great variety of articles, especially in a small shop where each man works on from one to ten separate jobs each day, I do not know whether it is best. I had recently a little experience in this matter myself, and found that my associates were somewhat averse to carrying out the ticket system, because in our shop, employing seventy or eighty men, each man having from one to ten jobs a day (averaging perhaps five), if separate tickets were used for all the recording of time, it averaged five tickets to each man per day, or thirty per week, which made the total very large. If there were a hundred men in the shop, there would be three thousand tickets. I have not any question in my mind that it *does* pay to handle that number of tickets, for the ease with which they can be assorted, compared with posting and rewriting in separate books; but when it comes to the amount of paper and necessary printing, I do not know about it. Of course, in the card system we only use ten tickets where a man does ten jobs, and only one where a man does one job in a day, and we waste no paper so far as that part of the ticket is concerned where the writing goes; but each one must have a certain space for a printed heading, and there must be the waste of paper due to that heading, and also the cost of the printing. If, however, you take one paper, or a larger card, for the recording of *one man's time* for a *week*, you have only one hundred such papers, instead of three thousand. A good deal of paper is of course wasted in cases where a man fills only one space out of ten provided. It is now a serious practical question in my mind which of the systems is best for my own particular case. I would like to ask Captain Metcalfe's opinion on this point—as to how great an evil is the necessary cost of extra paper and printing on the numerous tickets used where a small shop does a great variety of work and where each of the men has a great variety of jobs.

Capt. Metcalfe.—I will answer Mr. Smith by a reference to the saying about the honor which prophets receive in their own country. I have had to depend largely for experiments on what recognition my system might meet from private individuals and corporations. I got it up in the government works of which I had charge, but I have not had a full opportunity of trying it as I should like, and so cannot answer him explicitly. Of the general truth of the principles on which it is based I have no possible question. I began the trial of it at Frankford Arsenal, where we had a hundred and fifty or two hundred people. I generally had about a hundred orders under way, of different kinds, some little jobs and some quite important ones. There, instead of the unit card proposed, we had a card with ten horizontal lines on it, allowing for the reporting of ten jobs, if necessary, one for every hour in the day. The saving of labor there was very great. I was to hire a time clerk. He had two little boys to assist him in posting the cards. This kind of card made a very great change and helped very much. But still I did not get my reports in at the end of the month as quickly as I expected. I went out West. The selfish element entered still more largely into my facilities, for I had to do almost all the work myself. I was allowed a soldier, however, and by the use of these single card tickets he did everything in about an hour a day. We did not have as many men, but I had about sixty or eighty, and this soldier did all of the sorting and all of the computing, and I had everything ready at the first day of the month, a full account of everything done the month before, the cost of every order analyzed and balanced with the pay-roll. I made a computation the other day at the Watervliet Arsenal, West Troy, where I am stationed now, but where I have had nothing whatever to do with the management of the system. That is done by an officer who is my superior in rank, and who learned it from me at the Frankford Arsenal, and who has introduced it with some modifications. The card system is not followed there. The commanding officer there does not believe in having the workmen write on cards. I found that an average of a hundred and fifty men in a great many various capacities were making cotton duck equipments, harness, canteens, straps, steel and wooden gun carriages and a great many other parts of military furnishing. I found that about $1\frac{2}{10}$ to $1\frac{3}{10}$ orders per day were worked on per man. Some of the men went up to four, or five or six jobs a day—general utility men. Others work on the same jobs steadily day after day. I am very confident in saying that anybody who tries it will be very well satisfied with the great saving and the great readiness with which any desired result can be immediately attained. I think that answers Mr. Smith's question.

Mr. Smith.—Regarding the relative amount of paper and printing in the two systems I wanted to hear, if you please.

Capt. Metcalfe.—Of course in the independent card system there would be more paper and printing. As to the statement of Mr. Taylor, who is connected, I believe, with Messrs. William Sellers &

31

Co., to whom I am under many obligations, I think he somewhat confuses the order-tickets and the time-cards. The order-tickets are substantially such as he represents as being used in his works, although almost any convenient way of making the orders known to the workmen may be used. A bulletin-board will answer as well as anything, if nothing better can be found. Verbal transmission is the readiest, but of course it loses the character of a distinctive record. The order-tickets are not torn; they are simply passed out and then returned and the transaction is canceled. The only things which are torn are the labor cards, or service cards as I call them, which are torn off from the top of a book, so that, with the exception of the top one, they will always be reasonably clean. I have found no trouble with that. In my experience at the Benicia Arsenal the men kept them in little tin boxes outside their benches and filled them out as their work went on.

Then as to Mr. Anderson's remarks about the sheets getting dilapidated and the difficulty of keeping track of them; I found no trouble of that kind. I never found one of these cards to be lost. You do not lose them any more than you lose money. They are used as if to buy things with and go on from hand to hand until they get into the office, where they are all settled into their proper places. The receipt of the order ticket is indicated by each foreman's punch-marks on the duplicate retained by the superintendent, so that, having in his rack that ticket, the superintendent may see from a glance at the punch-marks upon it who has received this order, and in time that it has been completed by those whose numbers in the "completion" line he has punched out as their own cards come in completed.

All the record necessary is comprised on the original ticket.

Mr. Wm. Kent.—I have read a good deal about this subject the last six months, and also paid a great deal of attention to what has been brought before us here. No satisfactory solution of the question can be made by a desultory debate; there is so much difference of opinion as to its various details. I think it had better be referred to a committee who can report at a subsequent meeting of the Society. We might perhaps have a permanent committee on this subject instead of an economic section. I think such a committee should be composed of members who are in charge of manufacturing establishments, such as the three writers of the three papers presented to-day.

Mr. S. A. Hand.—In my business I have found it very useful in getting at the cost of work to use a blank such as is shown below:

COST OF...

Date.	Number of hours worked during the week.	Shop-expenses for the week.	Average rate of expenses per hour.	Number of hours worked on this job during the week.	Amount of wages for the week's work on this job.	Cost of the week's work on this job.
Total......						
Average...						

Cost of materials used—

Cost of machine work...
    Total cost...

In the first column is placed the date of the ending of the shop week. In the second is the total number of hours worked by all hands (excepting engineer and laborers) during the week. In the third column are put the shop expenses for one week. The shop expenses for one week, divided by the total number of hours worked, gives the average rate of expenses per hour per man employed. This is put in the fourth column. In the fifth column is put the number of hours worked on "this job" during the week, and in the sixth column is put the amount of wages paid for the week's work on this job. The average rate of expenses per hour per man employed multiplied by the number of hours worked on this job during the week, and the product added to the wages paid for the week's work on this job, gives us the total cost of the week's work on this job. This is put in the seventh or last column. Below, the sheet is ruled for the totals and averages of all the columns, which will in the course of time show the percentage of full time made by the men, the average expenses per hour, the average of wages paid to each hour worked, and the average value of worked turned out per dollar paid in wages.

Below the average space is a blank left for cost of material used in construction, which, added to the total cost of machine work, gives the total cost of the job. If a shop owner has a certain charge per hour for work he can soon tell whether that amount is paying him or not.

Mr. W. H. Doane.—I merely rise to ask the Captain to very kindly tell us how he arrived at the basis of cost; after he got the number of hours of labor how he arrived at the cost of the product.

Mr. Hawkins.—I quite agree with Mr. Towne in his advocacy of a committee to consider this subject; but I should hope that if a committee was appointed that they would not be confined strictly to the subjects of the papers as given. I am very much interested in that branch of the question which was touched upon by Mr. Partridge—making the workmen interested in the product—and my opinion is, from the experience I have had in the working of men, that there is no part of the question of economics of shop management that can begin to approach that, and if that can be extended to ordinary shops where piece work is impracticable, as it is in many cases, I think that is where we will accomplish the greatest saving that can be done by any means. We all know very well that the average mechanic, particularly such as have the care of automatic machines, planers, lathes, gear cutters, and last, though not least, the self-feeding drill, that they will waste time most abominably, and with the latter tool it is almost impossible to tell just how much they are wasting; and if you remonstrate with them, it is astonishing what tender solicitude they will have for the drill, and the dislike they have to render themselves liable to be considered as jeopardizing their future salvation in doing more than they ought to.

It is always the tendency of the average man, according to my observation, to do just as little as possible, particularly with automatic tools, and when you come to the question in a lathe or any self-feeding tool, of using one tooth on the feed-ratchet, or two, it is a very important question, and there is no part of the economics of the machine shop that can approach it in my opinion. I should like to see all that taken in by a committee.

Mr. Taylor.—I think Mr. Metcalfe has misunderstood me if he is of the opinion that I do not approve of the card system. I

thoroughly approve of the card system. We have tried it practically in our works for nearly ten years. It is simply the working
out of one part of the details of his system that I do not approve of.

His suggestion is, that each workman should have a book containing ten, or twenty, or a hundred or more cards, something like
a check book, and that each day he shall return one of those cards
to the office punched by the foreman of the shop, and my objection
was to that part of the system.

I think that the same card, the same check which he suggests as
being useful for conveying the time and the work done, and the
authority and so forth, to the central office, can be used to record a
great variety of other facts which are exceedingly interesting and
valuable. In point of fact in our works we use a great variety of
time cards, which proceed in our case first from the clerk to the
workman, and then from the workman back to the clerk.

We have at least, I should think, two hundred varieties of printed
cards, differing according to the information desired to be conveyed
from the workman to the office, all of them, however, containing to
a certain extent the same information; that is, each card conveys
the same information and other information besides as is recorded
on Mr. Metcalfe's blanks.

My criticism was that the information conveyed by his cards was
not sufficient. I fail also to see the advantage of using a punch as
described by Mr. Metcalfe. The initial of the foreman, or the
workman or the clerk is more rapidly made with a pen or pencil at
the same time as the writing is done on the card than it can be
with a punch, and it retains a certain amount of individuality.

Any one who gets hold of a punch can punch the authority for
doing work of any extent or variety that he chooses, but hand-writ-
ing is much more difficult to counterfeit.

Mr. Oberlin Smith.—I thoroughly believe in Capt. Metcalfe's
theory of the subject, and in his system as a whole, but I believe
with the other gentlemen here that some modifications may be
necessary for different shops. I confess I am a little alarmed at the
two or three thousand tickets a week which I might have to use if
I carried it out strictly, but I believe in a great many shops the
system exactly as it stands is just the thing. There may be other
shops where a modification making a card last a week instead of a
day for one workman would be better. There may be cases where
it would be better to put more than one job on the card, and there
are cases, as I said, where the Metcalfe system could be used in its

entirety. But all of this wants looking up, and in the happy future I hope that some committee or commission (perhaps of this Society) will have a chance to devise some systems of shop organization—not *one* system only, because we cannot apply one to all kinds of shops. The shops of this country want classifying into so many classes, and the best possible kind of organization for each will be ascertained only by careful study and by the collation of the experience of a great many persons.

In regard to the dirtying of the shop cards, I do not think it amounts to anything. In the concern with which I am connected we have allowed workmen to write directly on cards for a long time. We have never had any trouble with their being lost or dirtied or too much torn for practical use.

The point that Mr. Hawkins mentioned is an exceedingly important one, and one that occurs in shop economics more often than almost anything else. I really believe that in this country the lathes, planers, shapers, and drills are not running, on an average, over half way up to the capacity that they ought to in the matter of speeds and feeds. As he says, the universal tendency of the workmen is to run at too slow a speed, being afraid that the point of the tool will grind off. In our best shops you will see tools creeping along with a cut one one-hundredth of an inch deep and one one-hundredth of an inch wide. This waste of time is utterly unnecessary, and the only limit on depth or width of cutting ought to be the strength of the work. Where the work is weak, and therefore apt to break or bend, we cannot do thus, but ordinary work that is strong enough to resist the stresses ought to be worked up to the full belt power of the machine—that is, as far as *roughing* cuts are concerned. Finishing cuts must be more delicate.

Capt. Metcalfe.—So many suggestions have been made, it is rather hard to take them all up in order, and I may omit some.

Mr. Hawkins made a point about men. That suggests to me one point which I had not dwelt upon, which is that by making a workman start a record of what work he is doing, it gives him an interest in doing it rapidly from a feeling that it will be recorded somewhere in the office.

A gentleman asked me about the cost of production. The workman has to charge his time every day to some job so as to get paid for it. He is presumably disinterested in the cost of any particular job, so he tends to put it to the most probable one. We check his record by its verification by the foreman, and we make the probability greater by recording everything as nearly as possible at the time when it was done. I believe that the tendency will be to charge things,—in fact, I have noticed it myself,—to charge things as nearly as possible at the time when they are done. Then the record is shoved away and passed on to another person.

The general scheme is this, you stand in the center of your works, give your orders, and echoes come back to you telling what is going on. Now, these being physical items having individual numbers, to which labor and material are charged, they may be assorted in pigeon holes corresponding to the orders. They can be sorted from time to time during the progress of the work, so that, for example, the number of hours' work by operatives of the same class of wages being noted to get the cost of labor to date, you will merely have to add in those which have not been assorted. The differentiation can be carried still further, if necessary, so that by providing in the beginning for a more complete analysis, the number of days' or hours' work by each class of men on each component in that job may also be ascertained.

Mr. W. H. Doane.—My query had reference to the bases on which Capt. Metcalfe proposes to apportion the incidental expenses of an establishment.

Capt. Metcalfe.—The cost of work is made up, I believe, of the cost of labor, the cost of material, and its fair share of the incidental expenses of the establishment. I believe that the incidental expenses of an establishment should be distributed on the basis of the quantity of labor which the establishment holds, by what I call a cost factor. I find it is used in several shops, Mr. Smith's among others. I divide the incidental expenses of each department plus their fair share of the general expenses of the whole factory by the number of days' labor done in that department during the past year. That gives us, say, $1.25 per day. Rent, insurance, taxes, salaries, motive power, lighting, are all in the nature of facilities for the performance of labor. I once applied this method to the case of a stove factory, and with some satisfaction to those who heard me, I believe. If the price of iron goes up your incidental expenses do not increase. If your change of material were to be very great, say from an iron stove to a brass stove, your cost for motive power, etc., would not be any greater, so I leave material entirely out of the question and put these expenses with the cost of labor. But I distribute it according to the actual number of days' work irrespective of their cost. Poor labor costs more to watch it than dear labor. But if you attempted to divide your incidental expenses according to the cost of labor the difference would be the other way. You would have to charge more for dear labor than for cheap labor.

That is about all. As to Home Rule in the departments, that would be a question of locality. It is not necessary that everything should be run from the centralized power.

GAIN-SHARING

Henry R. Towne

CCCXLI.

G A I N - S H A R I N G .

BY HENRY R. TOWNE, STAMFORD, CONN.

(Member of the Society.)

WEBSTER defines *profit* as *the excess of value over cost*, and *gain* as meaning *that which is obtained as an advantage*. I have availed of this well-expressed though delicate distinction between the two terms, to coin a name for the system herein described, whereby to differentiate it from profit-sharing as ordinarily understood and practised.

Profit-sharing, as the term is now commonly used, implies a voluntary agreement, on the part of the principal in a business, to set aside some portion of the profits of his business for division among all or certain of his employees, as a stimulus to their zeal and industry. Thus understood, profit-sharing involves the participation of the employee in all the complex factors that affect the final result, or profit, of a business, including necessarily its *losses*, since these tend to impair, or may even extinguish, the profit. He thus becomes practically a partner, except that his participation in losses is limited to the surrender of his share in anticipated profits, and does not involve any impairment of his personal capital.

It follows, therefore, in most cases of profit-sharing, that the interest of each participator in the profit fund is largely affected by the actions of others whom he cannot control or influence, and that what he may earn or save for the common good may be lost by the mismanagement or extravagance of others. For example, let us suppose the case of a trader who buys and sells a certain staple, such as cotton, and who, having two clerks, entrusts to one of them the purchasing of the staple, and to the other the business of selling it to the customers of the house. Obviously here the amount of profit will depend partly upon the ability of the buyer to purchase material of the proper quality at the lowest market rate, and partly upon the ability of the seller to dispose of it promptly at the highest obtainable prices. If each does his share well, a large profit may result; while if either fails in his part there may be no profit, or even a loss, no matter how well the other may have performed his part. But it does not follow that the work of either or both will determine the question of profit, for unexpected changes in the market may neutralize the best plans and cause loss, or may result in large profit in spite of unskilful management.

Let us now suppose the case of a manufacturer who, in addition to buying the raw material, converts it into a finished product before selling it, and who voluntarily concedes to the operatives of the manufacturing department of his business, as well as to his chief assistants, a participation in its profits. The factors affecting the profit fund now become more complex, and may be divided into several distinct groups, as follows :

1. Those contributed or controlled by the owner or principal,— such as capital, plant, character of buildings, machinery and organization ; and, to a greater or less degree, the skill, experience, industry, and ability of the owner so far as he personally manages the business.

2. Those influenced by the mercantile staff,—the buyer and the selling agent in the case supposed.

3. Those determined by causes beyond the control of the principal and his agents; such as fluctuations in cost of raw material or in the market value of the finished product, the rate of interest, losses by bad debts, etc.

4. Those influenced by the workmen or operatives ; such as care of property, economy in the use of material and supplies, and, chiefly, efficiency in the use of machinery and employment of labor.

Now it is obvious that while the operatives may influence the items in the fourth or last group to an extent which may be large, or even controlling, in determining the question of profit or loss, they have little control—and in most cases none whatever—over the items specified in the other three groups ; and that to admit them to participation in the net results of the whole business, while commendable as an act of generosity, is not defensible either as an equitable adjustment of the complex and often conflicting interests involved, nor as a theoretically correct solution of an economic problem.

The right solution of this problem will manifestly consist in allotting to each member of the organization an interest in that portion of the profit fund which is or may be affected by his individual efforts or skill, and in protecting this interest against diminution resulting from the errors of others, or from extraneous causes not under his control. Such a solution, while not simple, is attainable under many circumstances, and attainable by methods which experience has shown to be both practical and successful.

This resolution of the profit fund into component parts obviates many of the crudities in, and objections to, profit-sharing in its common form, but still leaves untouched another feature which is wrong in theory and often objectionable in practice, namely, the surrender by the principal of any portion of his legitimate profits without the assurance of an equivalent return from those on whom he bestows it. This, as said above, may be commendable as an act of charity, but as a solution of the problem in question it is neither complete nor accurate. Moreover, mere charity to those who do not need it is a doubtful good, and among intelligent and self-respecting men is not always relished. Certainly the problem we are considering will be best solved if it can be so formulated that the element of gratuity or charity, of giving without tangible consideration, can be eliminated, and that, as presented to the employee, it becomes an invitation from the principal that they should enter into an industrial partnership, wherein each will retain, unimpaired, his existing equitable rights, but will share with the other the benefits, if any are realized, of certain new contributions made by each to the common interest. For example, to recur to our former case, let us suppose that the wages of the operatives are already fairly adjusted according to the prevailing scale, so that for the employer to offer them a portion of his profits without a guaranty of return would be equivalent to his giving them more than the fair market value of their services; while if, under this inducement, they gave him better or more work than before, they would not receive fair recompense in case, by reason of causes beyond their control, his business yielded no profit. But let us suppose, further, that the principal, wishing to enlist the self-interest of his employees to augment the profits of the business, should offer to the operatives a proposition somewhat as follows :

"I have already ascertained the cost of our product in labor, supplies, economy of material, and such other items as you can influence. I will undertake to organize and pay for a system whereby the cost of product in these same items will be periodically ascertained, and will agree to divide among you a certain portion (retaining myself the remainder) of any gain, or reduction of cost, which you may effect by reason of increased efficiency of labor, or increased economy in the use of material, or both; this arrangement not to disturb your rates of wages, which are to continue, as at present, those generally paid for similar services."

Can there be any question as to the inherent fairness and accuracy of this solution of our problem, or any doubt as to its cheerful acceptance by intelligent labor? As to the latter point an emphatic answer has already been given by actual experience; as to the former a reply will be attempted in what follows.

The system for which I have adopted the designation of "Gain-sharing" aims to recognize and provide for the conditions typified by the foregoing supposititious case, and to afford a basis for allotting to the employees in a business a share in the gain or benefit accruing from their own efforts, without involving in the account the general profits or losses of the business. The system is now in actual use as affecting some 300 employees, has been in operation more than two years, and is demonstrated to be practical and beneficial. It has been applied to nearly one half the divisions of a large and unusually varied industry, and will ultimately be extended to nearly all. As soon as understood by the employees, it is liked, and those not working under it in the instance referred to are desirous that it should be extended to include them. Its most obvious application is to productive industries, especially those whose product is of a simple or uniform kind; but it may be adapted to many others, and also to the business of large mercantile houses. It is equally applicable to cases where labor is employed either by the piece, by the day, or by contract, and in no way impairs the existing freedom of the relation between employer and employee, but tends to confer substantial benefit on both sides.

The basis or starting-point of the system is an accurate knowledge of the present cost of product (or, in the case of a mercantile business, the cost of operating it), stated in terms which include the desired factors, that is, those which can be influenced or controlled by the employees who are to participate in the result, and which exclude all other factors. In some cases the previous method of accounting or book-keeping may have been such as to supply this information, in which case the gain-sharing system can be easily and promptly organized. In others the existing books may contain the record from which the desired information can be digested and compiled. Where no such record exists, however, the only safe method consists in devising and putting into action a system of accounts which will furnish the desired *data*, and in awaiting the accumulation thereby of information which, being based upon the operations of a reasonably long period,—usually from six to twelve months,—will constitute a fair mean or average.⟩

The factors which should be included in, and those which should be excluded from, the account, will vary with circumstances, each particular case having to be considered by itself. As a general rule it may be stated that, in the case of an account affecting the operatives in a producing or manufacturing business, the following items should be *included*, viz. : labor at cost, raw material, measured by quantity only (for which purpose an arbitrary fixed price may be assumed) ; incidental supplies, such as oil, waste, tools and implements, at cost ; cost of power, light, and water, where means exist for correctly measuring them (for which purpose it often pays to provide local meters) ; cost of renewals and repairs of plant ; and, finally, the cost of superintendence, clerk hire, etc., incident to the department covered by the system. In like manner the following items should be *excluded*, viz. : market values of raw material (which are liable to fluctuation) ; general expenses, whether relating to management of works or to commercial administration, and, in general, all items over which the operatives can exercise no control or economy. Finally, the credit side of the account should be determined by the amount or volume of product measured by a scale of values fixed in advance, and based upon facts previously ascertained. For example, if, in a given case, it has been determined by the experience of several years that the present cost of product, measured by such items as are covered by the inclusive list above stated, is, say, one dollar ($1) per unit of product, then the gain-sharing proposition might be formulated as follows : the principal would say to the employees, in substance, " I will organize the system, will assume the cost of book-keeping and other expenses incident to it, and will provide all the facilities reasonably required to assist you in reducing the cost of product ; I will credit the account with the output at the cost price heretofore obtaining, namely $1 per unit, and will charge it with the items in the inclusive list ; if at the end of the year the credits exceed the charges, I will divide the resulting *gain*, or reduction in cost, with you, retaining myself one portion,—say one half,—and distributing the other portion among you *pro rata* on the basis of the wages earned by each during the year." Supposing, then, that at the end of the year it was found that the cost per unit of product had been reduced from $1 to 95 cents, that the total gain thus resulting was $800; and that the aggregate wages paid during the year had been $10,000. One-half of the gain would be $400, which would equal 4 per cent. on the wages fund, so that each operative would be entitled to a dividend of 4 per cent. on his earnings during the year. This is equivalent to two weeks' extra wages, no mean addition to any income, and amounting, even in the case of a laborer earning $1.50 per day, to a cash dividend of $18 at the end of the year.

In the practical application of the system several important details have to be determined, for which no general rule can be laid down. Of these the most important is the question of the division of the gain or profit between employer and employees. In each of the twenty-one gain-sharing contracts which I have thus far instituted, it has seemed proper to make this division an equal one,—one-half to the principal and one-half to the operatives,—and the results thus far have justified the rule and proved generally satisfactory to both parties to the contract. Obviously, however, different circumstances may justify or require a different basis of division.

Another important question is the share of the profit fund or *gain* apportioned to the foreman, overseer, or contractor having immediate control of the operatives interested under the system. Where such person is employed under salary he may share *pro rata* with the operatives, but as this would tend to diminish his share with any increase of responsibility due to the need of an increased number of subordinates, I prefer to allot to him a definite part of the profit fund. Assuming fifty to be the average number of employees under one foreman, I regard ten to fifteen per cent of the profit fund as about the proper allotment to the foreman, leaving forty to thirty-five per cent for his subordinates, where fifty per cent is retained by the employer.

As the foreman has more power and control than any subordinate, it is proper that his interest should be larger, and it is expedient, also, in adjusting his total compensation, to make a considerable fraction of it contingent upon the results of his work. Where the "contract system" of work prevails, I have adopted the rule of paying the contractor, like his helpers, by the hour; his "basis rate," or rate per hour, being determined by adding together the three following factors, viz.: (1) his value as a workman, usually that of his best helpers; (2) one half cent per hour for each completed year of service as contractor, in recognition of increased value due to experience; and (3) a figure representing a very small but definite percentage on the aggregate amount of his contract earnings, in recognition of the fact that his responsibility varies somewhat with the volume of work under his control. The first of these items is usually constant; the second causes a slight annual increase in the " basis rate;" while the third tends to increase the rate when the volume of business is large, and to reduce it when business falls off. The percentage of the profit fund or " gain " allotted to a contractor may be larger, proportionately, than to a salaried foreman, depending upon his duties, his liability for quality of product, and the amount of his " basis rate " or hourly wages. As in the former case, however, it is desirable that a considerable fraction of his total compensation should be derived from the profit fund, and thus be contingent upon the results of his work.

A third point to be considered is the basis of participation on which the dividend to the operatives shall be apportioned among them. The simplest plan, and the one which I have adopted in practice, is to distribute the total profit fund allotted to the operatives on the basis of the actual wages earned by each during the year, including in the account everyone employed during that time, even if for one day only. If a dividend is earned it is not payable until the year is closed, when it is paid in cash, in the same manner as the regular wages, but enclosed in a special " dividend envelope," on which is stated the total annual wages of the recipient, and the rate and amount of his dividend. The rules should provide for the disposition of unclaimed dividends, which may very properly go into the treasury of a mutual benefit fund, if such an organization exists, and should also be carefully framed with reference to local laws, in order to avoid unforeseen liabilities and complications.

It has been found feasible, and very beneficial, to have posted in each room or department where the gain-sharing system is in force, a suitable blank, preferably under glass, on which can be entered each month the net results of the system during the preceding month, and including a statement of the *rate* of dividend earned since the beginning of the contract year. The stimulus thus given to the interest of the employees is very marked.

Another point of much importance is the question of the length of time during which a contract for " gain-sharing " shall continue without modification. Its inception is voluntary with the employer, and he may impose on the contract any conditions he sees fit, since its whole purport is to tender to the employee an interest in excess of his stipulated wages, from which it is expected that he will gain an increase of his compensation, but under which he cannot possibly suffer loss. Such a contract, however, when once definitely entered into, is, like other contracts, only amenable to revision by the joint consent of both parties to it. It is important, therefore, that its provisions be carefully considered in advance.

The length of time which it is desirable to adopt for a gain-sharing contract depends greatly upon the conditions of the case. As already explained, the starting-point of the system is a knowledge of the previous *cost of product*, the " gain " or increased economy in this constituting the fund out of which the increased compensation to labor is to be paid. When, therefore, the cost of product is already accurately known, a gain-sharing contract may safely be made for a considerable length of time, whereas, when the cost is not well known, it is better to fix its terms for a shorter period, in order that they may be revised when the necessary information has been obtained. The best results will be obtained, however, when the contract is definitely fixed for a reasonably long period, say from three to five years, or even longer. A necessary element in the case is the adoption of a " contract price " for each article to be produced, by which, as previously explained, the credit side of the account may be determined. At the beginning of a contract the employer obviously has the right to adopt whatever " contract prices " he pleases, since their purpose is merely to serve as a basis from which to compute the " gain " in which he voluntarily tenders participation to the employees, and since the contract does not diminish the obligation of the employer to pay each employee his stipulated wages. Presumably the employer will adopt reasonably low contract prices, that is, closely approximating to previous cost ; because to do otherwise would be prejudicial to his own interests, although to fix them on too low a scale would defeat the object of the system by leaving no opportunity for " gain," and hence no stimulus to increased efficiency of the employee. In like manner, at the expiration of a contract, the option and right reverts to the employer of revising the " contract prices " before offering a renewal of the contract ; in which event, if during the previous term the cost of product has been considerably reduced, he will presumably (although this is not always the wisest course) proportionately reduce the contract prices. If, therefore, the contract period be short, the employee will naturally ask himself whether it is to his interest, for the sake of a small increase of compensation during that period, to make increased exertion in view of the fact that, at the end of the period, the employer will probably again reduce prices to a point where, in order to increase his earnings, the employee would have to exert himself even more than at first. If, however, the contract price be definitely fixed for a long period, the employee can afford, for the sake of present gain, to disregard this question as one only affecting a somewhat remote future, and to use his best efforts and intelligence to effect a reduction in the cost of product. As a result of this the employer will be able, when the opportunity for a revision of prices arises, to make a larger reduction than he would probably attain in the same time under the plan of frequent revisions, and can also then afford to act more liberally toward the employees in the matter. In my judgment, therefore, both parties will usually be benefited by having a long contract period in all cases where the previous cost of product is well known, and where no radical change of product or methods is likely to occur.

The simplest application of the gain-sharing system is to cases where work has already been done by contract,—that is, where one person, employed for the purpose, is paid for the finished product *by the piece*, the wages of his helpers being charged against his account; and it can be readily organized in any case where the nature of the product is such as to adapt it to being thus done " by contract." In this connection it is proper to note that the contract method, whether under the gain-sharing system or not, is entirely compatible with "piece-work," that is, an arrangement whereby each operative is paid for his individual product by the piece instead of by day's wages. In this case the amount of piece-work earnings is charged against the contract account in the same manner as the wages of persons employed by the day or hour, and is treated in the same manner as other earnings in computing the dividend of each operative under a gain-sharing contract. In corroboration of this statement I may mention that I have already adopted gain-sharing in several cases where the work was previously and is still done under the "contract" system, and in which, also, the piece-work system has since been largely applied. We thus have the three systems of gain-sharing, contract-work, and piece-work, all co-existing harmoniously, and all contributing to a common result.

Again, in the case of a foundry, the gain-sharing system can be easily and advantageously applied. Here economy of material as well as efficiency of labor is largely under control of the operatives, and should be made a factor in the account. This can be accomplished by basing the "cost of product" upon the ascertained results of a previous period, labor and miscellaneous items of small supplies being charged up at actual cost, and fuel and metal being charged according to an arbitrary scale of fixed prices, which may conveniently be determined by adopting the average market rate during the previous year, or at its close. The arbitrary values for material which are thus adopted are then incorporated in the gain-sharing contract, and remain unchanged during its period. The "contract prices" for finished product are deduced from the actual results of the preliminary period, the cost of material being calculated by extending the actual quantities at the arbitrary prices per pound or other unit which may have been adopted for the proposed contract, the employer using his discretion as to how close the contract prices should be to previous actual costs. Where the foundry product is of varied character, a separate price is fixed for each class of castings, and a record kept of the output of each.

Gain-sharing may thus be adapted to industries of almost any kind in which it is feasible, by reasonable expenditure, to differentiate those elements of cost which can be influenced by the persons who are to participate in the resulting gain from those which are beyond such influence or control. Careful and intelligent consideration must be given to properly adapting the system to the varied circumstances and details of each case; and the experience of several renewals of a gain-sharing contract, each accompanied by the modifications and improvements which are the outcome of experience, may be needed to attain the highest results. In my own experience I have failed, in a few cases, properly to adjust the conditions, and hence have seen the first year close with an apparent loss instead of a gain. In such cases a careful analysis of the operations of the year will usually explain the cause of disappointment and indicate the remedy. The first year of a contract for gain-sharing is apt to be disappointing to its promoter, owing to lack of interest, faith, and comprehension on the part of the employees. These all vanish, however, under the convincing argument of a *cash dividend*, and after the first of these has been paid there is usually a marked increase of interest in the plan.

Appended hereto are several papers illustrative of the working of the system in actual practice. The first of these—Appendix A—

gives the results obtained in the case of a number of the contracts to which I have applied the gain-sharing system, two of these covering a period of two years each. All of the others are now running on the second year, but only the results of the first year are here stated. The "contract prices" adopted for these gain-sharing accounts were in some cases the actual previous costs, but in a majority of cases the contract prices were fixed at rates which were a reduction of from ten to twenty per cent., and in one case of thirty per cent. from previous costs. These reductions were made advisedly, and only in cases where there was good reason to believe that increased effort would result in very considerable reductions of costs. In most cases the results have justified the reductions, and even on the basis of the new prices the contracts have yielded fair profits or dividends.

Appendix B is a transcript of one of the monthly exhibits mentioned above as being posted in the room or shop where the system is in force. These figures were inserted in the blank, month by month during the year, and gave information to the employees of the results of their work as affecting their interests under the gain-sharing contract. In this case the proportion of gain allotted to helpers was twenty-five per cent., and the net result of the operations for the year yielded a dividend to them of 5.7 per cent. on their wages or earnings during the year.

Appendix C shows the rules governing the application of the gain-sharing system to the iron foundry in the works of the Yale & Towne Manufacturing Company, at Stamford, Connecticut. Where the system is applied to a shop or department in which contract work obtains, the rules require modification in certain details, but are substantially the same in principle as those given herewith. In all cases the rules will require careful adaptation to the details of the particular work to which they relate, and to the methods of shop management and organization which are in use.

APPENDIX A.

Contract No.	Term.	Helpers' earnings.	Gain or loss.	Helpers' share.	Rate of dividend.
1	5 years.	$13,080 43	$3,388 53	$850 18	.065 %
2	5 "	9,216 87	* 37 59	. . .	. . .
3	5 "	3,666 34	840 05	208 98	.057 %
4	3 "	4,936 54	573 58	148 09	.03 %
5	5 "	910 22	* 48 52	. . .	. . .
7	3 "	3,861 28	537 72	134 43	.035 %
8	3 "	1,012 92	447 59	111 42	.11 %
9	3 "	419 55	109 04	27 27	.065 %
10	5 "	17,696 47	1,256 37	3:8 53	.018 %
15	5 "	728 53	358 20	89.62	.123 %

SECOND YEAR.

1		$14,096 05	$3,251 04	$817 56	.058 %
3		3,732 21	1,027 20	261 15	.07 %

* Losses.

APPENDIX B.

The Yale & Towne Manufacturing Co.
Monthly Accounts Relating to Contract No. 3—1887.

MONTHS.	TOTAL PROFIT FOR MONTH.	PROFITS FROM BEGINNING OF YEAR.			MONTHLY CHARGES FOR TOOLS.	MONTHLY CHARGES FOR SUPPLIES.
		Total amount.	25% belonging to helpers.	Percentage on wages.		
January	* $45 52				$55 84	$3 95
February	85 72	$40 20	$10 05	.017	46 85	2 97
March	115 53	155 73	38 93	.039	78 13	7 62
April	98 48	254 21	63 55	.046	35 57	5 98
May	* 51 46	202 75	50 69	.0307	37 16	1 75
June	182 90	385 65	96 41	.0505	26 66	2 04
July	9 12	394 77	98 69	.046	17 25	2 74
August	76 12	470 89	117 72	.049	27 10	2 02
September	8 64	479 53	119 88	.044	44 20	3 14
October	114 76	594 29	148 57	.0499	56 96	6 27
November	* 94 72	499 57	124 89	.0378	58 30	75
December	340 48	840 05	210 01	.057	27 30	4 56
Totals for Year	$840 05	$840 05	$210 00	.057	$5 1 32	$43 79

* Losses.

APPENDIX C.

The Yale & Towne Mfg. Company, Stamford, Conn. Rules for "Gain-sharing" System in Iron Foundry, December, 1887.

1.—Contract Period.

The present contract between the company and the employees of the Foundry will cover a period from December 1st, 1887, to December 1st, 1888, and will be subject to revision after the latter date.

2.—The System.

The "gain-sharing" system has been in operation during 1887 throughout the greater part of Dept. A, where some 200 men are now at work under it. Its essential principle is this: that out of each $100 of savings or "gain" in the cost of product, in labor and supplies, the Company retains only $50, the other $50 being divided among the employees in the Department. To accomplish this the Company agrees to organize the method of operation, to keep the necessary accounts, and in general to facilitate matters so far as it reasonably can; the employees, on the other hand, agree to use their best efforts to increase the efficiency of their work, to economize in the use of supplies and material, and in general to do their share towards reducing the cost of finished products.

3.—Contract Prices.

To establish a basis by which to measure the saving or gain effected, the following plan has been adopted. The average prices for metal and fuel which prevailed during the past six months have been carefully ascertained, and these prices have been adopted for the contract period; applying these prices to the product of the Foundry for the past six months, all other items of labor and supplies being extended at their actual amounts, the cost per pound of castings of each class during the past six months has been ascertained; the prices thus ascertained are adopted as the *basis prices* for the contract period.

4.—Contract Profit or Gain.

At the close of each month of the contract period the cost of castings produced during the month will be ascertained by charging up the metal and fuel at the *fixed prices* adopted as above, and charging all other items, including wages and supplies, at actual cost. If the cost of castings thus ascertained is less than the *basis cost* determined as above, the difference between the two will be the saving or gain for the month. The results of each month's operations will be posted in the Foundry for the information of the employees.

5.—DIVISION OF PROFITS.

Within thirty days after the close of the contract year the total amount of saving or gain will be divided as follows:

Fifty per cent. will be retained by the Company.

Ten per cent. will be allotted to the Foreman of the Foundry.

Forty per cent. will be distributed among the employees of the Foundry in the proportion of the actual wages earned by each during the contract year.

6.—WAGES RATES.

The wages of each employee will be fixed, as heretofore, by the Foreman of the Foundry, who will continue to have full discretion in the employment and discharge of the help required, and in the direction of their work.

7.—PAYMENT OF PROFITS.

Each employee will be entitled to his pro rata share of the profits, whether he has worked during the whole year or only a portion thereof. Any share of profits belonging to those who may honorably leave the Company's service during the year will be forwarded to them, provided they shall have given proper information as to their address. Any profits due to employees, and not claimed within three months after the close of any yearly contract period, will thereby become forfeited; all sums thus forfeited will be paid over by the Company to the Yale & Towne Mutual Benefit Society.

8.—PIECE WORK.

Wherever feasible the system of piece-work will be employed, the piece rates being fixed by the Foreman subject to approval by the Company. All employees, whether working by the day or by the piece, will be entitled to their proportionate share of the annual profits on the basis of the actual wages earned by each.

9.—Foundry Supplies.

The Foundry account will be charged with all supplies furnished by the Company. The items so charged will include metals, fuel, sand, sieves, files, shovels, oil, waste, brooms, repairs, and, in general, everything consumed in the Foundry.

The supplies on hand at the beginning of the contract period will be charged to the Foundry account, and those on hand at the end of the year will be credited to the same account.

10.—Guaranty.

The Company guarantees the payment to the employees of the Foundry of the regular wages earned by each, on day work or piece work, irrespective of whether this contract shows a profit or not.

11.—Conditions.

The effect of the system being to give every workman employed under this contract a participation in the profits resulting from it, it is hereby stipulated, as a condition of the employment of each and every person engaged under this system, that, in consideration of the interest assigned him in the profits of the contract, all claim thereto shall be forfeited by him in the event of his discharge by reason of misconduct or incompetency, or in the event of his combining with others in any way to disturb or affect the relations between the Company and its employees. This provision in no way curtails the right of each employee to negotiate with the Company, through the Foreman, in regard to his own rate of wages, nor does it in any way impair the title of each employee to his proportionate share of the profits in the event of his honorably leaving the Company's service, whether at its desire or his own.

12.—Shop Rules.

All employees will continue to be governed by the Shop Rules of the Company, which are hereby referred to and made a part of this contract and agreement.

DISCUSSION.

The President, Henry R. Towne.—Supplementing what is stated in the paper itself, I may say that since writing it I have ascertained that during the year ending April 30th, in a case where the system is in operation, the total profit or gain resulting from the operation of this system was $8,062, one-half of which was retained by the principal and the other half distributed among the operatives. The rates of dividends to the employees were approximately the same as those indicated in Appendix A of the paper, which range from a minimum of about one per cent. to a maximum of twelve per cent.; the mean is about four or five per cent.

If there are any members present who have in any way experimented with profit-sharing, or participation, or any kindred method of interesting employees in industrial works in the outcome of their work, it would be interesting to the membership to have the result of their experience.

Prof. Denton.—I hardly feel competent to speak about a subject of this kind, in the presence of the knowledge that a good deal of actual experience is necessary to be considered regarding it. But I feel that this paper is so admirable that one or two thoughts may be permitted. We all probably remember that this subject came out at the Washington meeting, and that our President then discussed the paper that was there presented, and made the matter interesting by detailing the extent to which this idea had already become prevalent in other countries with success; and considerable interest was evidenced on the part of other members. He promised us at that time to give us such a paper as this, and now keeps his promise in a very valuable way. The importance of the subject, I believe, can hardly be over-estimated; for I am informed that the idea is looked upon with favor by the labor organizations, in which case it may be likely to come before any manufacturer at any time. The idea in my mind regarding it is that the gain together with profit-sharing contains a distinct element of favor as compared with piece work. We all know, if a man is earning by the day, on a certain work which is uniform, certain wages at so many pieces in a day, and is apparently doing all that he knows how, and all that we know how to ask him to do, we know that if we put his work on piece price so adjusted that it is supposed that he will just about make wages, he will at once proceed to make double wages. In some way he will turn out so many pieces that his wages will double, and the tendency on the part of the employer is, the next time the piece work adjustment comes around, to readjust the piece price so that the man will more nearly approximate his former

day wages. That has been going on for many years in many
establishments; and I believe that constant reduction in piece
prices, and all the time getting from the workman more than he
originally did, has resulted in a sour state of mind on the part
of the latter; he thinks that the piece work system has been
used to his disadvantage, and I can easily see that the question
must arise in an establishment that is carrying on piece work like
that of Mr. Towne's: How can we at once get the workman to
squeeze a little more out of himself and at the same time be good-
natured in doing it? A method of doing that is represented certainly in this idea of gain or profit sharing. I believe that the
fact that the workman sees in it something to encourage him to
go beyond piece work is likely to bring out a much better state of
feeling between employer and employee than existed on the piece
work system. I have seen the idea carried out on a small scale.
I have in mind a manufactory which organized itself in a small
way, and drew to it, through the acquaintance of the proprietor,
certain excellent men, so skilful that they were able to earn the
very highest wages. They went with him and expected that he
would prosper, but he was barely able to drag along; business
did not succeed, work was not available, and there was every motive to those men to leave him. They could go to more prosperous concerns where they would be likely to do better. I have
seen this idea of gain-sharing carried out there on a very small
scale, holding those men year after year. It was not the money
they made, so much as the idea that they were interested with the
proprietor in the profits of the concern. I have tried the same
thing on a small scale in this way: We have instructors in our
shops at Hoboken, in pipe fitting, blacksmithing and machinists'
work. We are all the time extending our courses and asking those
men to do a little more. We also often have certain experimental
tests to perform for the general public, and we organized a department of tests which is presided over by the President, and
any work coming in is given to the men best fitted to do it. Nine-
tenths of the work naturally falls upon those mechanics in some
way. We want them to do this work and not sacrifice the least
point in the efficiency of the instruction. We ask them to carry
out what they were hired to do and at the same time enable the
college to earn a little money. There is no idea that so nicely fits
the case as dividing a portion of the profits, and we have found
that such a plan is working very nicely. Our men may be

called upon to take hold of any outside job, and work late hours or squeeze it in between times, and yet the system of instruction does not suffer, and the amount of profit, though small, is sufficient to make them feel it is worth while to put forth this exertion. This is very easy when you have a few men ; but when you have hundreds of men, I can see that difficulties multiply enormously, because there will be some black sheep, who thinks that he does not get enough, and he will communicate his irritation to his fellows, and it may lead to strikes. When it is done on such a scale as Mr. Towne has done it, and as well as he has done it, certainly great advantage must result, and great pains have been taken in his establishment ; and I wish to testify to my appreciation of this fact.

The President, Mr. H. R. Towne.—In connection with this subject I wish to mention a book, which has just been published, which has more information, better stated, on the subject of profit-sharing than any other book in the English language. The best one we had heretofore was one by Sedley Taylor, an English book, which is not as complete as one or two publications in German and French. But the Rev. Dr. Gilman of Boston has, during the past year, prepared and published a book which is just out now under the title of " Profit Sharing between Employer and Employee," in which he has brought together all of the facts which are of interest in this whole subject of profit-sharing, commencing with a rapid review of previous conditions existing between employers and employees which departed at all from the simple wages basis ; then follows a discussion of the reasons why the simple wages system is no longer satisfactory now and that something else has so to supersede it, and then a very thorough presentation of all the known cases of profit-sharing all over the world. France is the country where the system first took root to any extent, in the Maison Leclaire in Paris, and where it has been most largely practised, and French experience is the fullest and most interesting. The Germans have done a good deal with it. The English took it up some twenty-five years ago, and in two very striking cases put it into extensive and very successful use ; each of them was finally abandoned within six or eight years, from causes having no direct connection with the question whether profit-sharing is a good or bad thing in itself; but the result of its abandonment was unfortunately to put the whole thing back very much in England, so that nothing more has been done there in that line until lately, when it has again been taken hold of. In this country, within the last three years, profit-sharing has been started in twenty or thirty different establishments scattered all over the country; and Mr. Gilman, in his book, has brought together the facts, so far as proprietors were willing to give them, in all of the cases in each of the countries named, and also in Switzerland and Italy. His last two chapters constitute a *résumé* or summary of the results everywhere, stating plainly the failures where they have occurred, and so far as possible accounting for them. To anyone who contemplates giving thought to the subject of profit-sharing, or any modification of it, Mr. Gilman's book will be an invaluable aid.

In my own opinion the time is coming very rapidly when some readjustment of the relations of labor and capital has got to be made, not necessarily by reason of the demands of labor organizations, but simply, if we disregard all questions of philanthropy or sympathy, from motives of self-interest on the part of the employer. Some better method of bringing out of men the best that is in them in doing their work must be adopted. It is a fact which we all realize, of course, although we sometimes forget it, that the supreme factor in human endeavor is self-interest, and that any plan whereby we bring in self-interest as an agent to influence the workman, will induce him to take hold in a degree and manner that nothing else will approach, and that any system, such as the simple wages method, which entirely ignores self-interest and gives a daily stipend to a man whether he does much or little, is certainly a very incomplete and very unsatisfactory adjustment of the problem. I believe that all large employers of labor will find this subject one of profit and of interest to take up in the near future, and that the outcome should be the development of a large fund of experience which will aid others who desire to go into it. The meetings of this Society since they have been opened to the discussion of economic problems will make a very proper place for the presentation of data relating to such matters, and I know that it is the desire of many members that experiences of this kind, when obtained by the members, may and should appear in our Transactions.

Prof. Wood.—I wish to ask, Mr. President, if your experience makes you feel that this can be carried into a great variety of business transactions—where a manufacturer is making a variety of things?

The President.—In answer to Prof. Wood's question I may say that the system is in operation now under twenty-one different contracts, and is to be extended to others, and that no two of those twenty-one contracts relate to the same product ; a number of them somewhat allied products involving a different group of men, different kinds of machines and different work, but quite a number of them are totally distinct products, including two foundries, one on iron work and another on brass and bronze, several wood-working operations, one which largely involves chemical operations, and another which includes the work of a large wheel-finishing room. The others are chiefly machine shop work. I think this is a thorough answer to the question, and it is my conviction about it, that the system is applicable to almost any industrial product that I know of.

Prof. Wood.—I wish also, in order to cover the ground, to ask whether the success of it will not depend largely upon the managers. You speak of securing the self-interest of the laborer. Now, if the business is not so managed as to secure a dividend, I would ask whether the interest would not depart from the workman in such cases and so be a failure. Even if there are only exceptional cases of failure, it does not invalidate the system by any means ; but does not very much depend upon the managers in making it successful?

Mr. Chas. H. Parker.—I am glad to see such papers as the one presented by Mr. Towne on the question of gain-sharing. I think in the present condition of mind of the laboring people, as well as of the manufacturers, it is one of the problems that needs attention fully as much as any of the problems connected with the manufacturing industries. It has been my fortune for over something like fifteen years to be in a position where this problem has been brought to me very forcibly. I have found that nearly all the difficulties and troubles that arise regarding a fair and just arrangement, you may say, have a starting point in the selfishness of human nature. But I can say from experience that I never yet have seen any reason to lose faith ; that where a spirit of justice and fairness is used on the part of the manufacturer, sooner or later, although not always at first, the same spirit has been shown by the workmen ; and as a whole the results have not weakened my confidence in the final adoption on both sides of just and fair ideas. There are questions constantly arising that cannot at first be foreseen. Self-interest will often cause the workmen to take a

position that the manufacturer is the one who seeks to do them
an injustice; but if the proprietor meets that spirit with fair, open
treatment and intercourse, I will say that in that case I have found
generally on the part of men a disposition to meet him in the same
way. I have one case in mind of a question that arose in regard
to work that was let to an individual contractor who hired his
workmen and made his individual bargains with them, the actual
cost being paid by the proprietors as suggested in Mr. Towne's
paper. During the progress of the work the establishment was
destroyed by fire. The contractor had unfinished work in process
of manufacture unsettled for, something like seven or eight hundred dollars. The question came up, How shall this matter of
loss to the contractor for the interest he had in the contract (the
loss of his profits that were partially wiped out by the fire) be
settled? It would seem in the first case as though it would be
plain enough that his risk on undelivered work, so to speak, was
of the same nature as the risk of any manufacturer on undelivered
machinery or materials, that he had not covered by insurance, but
it is hard work sometimes to make a workman look at things in
just that light. In this case I did not attempt to decide as to
what was right. I simply stated that it seemed to me that the
contractor was obliged to carry a certain amount of risk on that
portion of his contract work that was not settled for, and left it
for him in common with one or two other contractors who were
involved in the same way to talk it over among themselves, and
to my surprise they voluntarily came forward and said that after
thinking the matter over they decided that, to be secured against
any risk of that kind, it was their duty to be insured, either
through the regular channels of insurance on unfinished products
in process, or to have some understanding with the manufacturer
by which he would reimburse them by paying a certain amount
for the risk. And the matter was finally settled by their coming
to the agreement that the risk did properly belong to them. I
will say, in regard to this question of the constant reduction of
contract prices, I find that that is easily regulated if attention is
given in the first place to investigating as to what is a fair profit
for a man to make. We will say of a contractor who is able
to manage twelve or fifteen men himself, What is a fair compensation for that man's service? Is it expecting any too much that
he should make five dollars a day? By careful investigation of
the question, it is easy to arrive at what is the marketable value of

the services of such a man. Now, if the material exists to judge how many days' labor enter into the construction, and what the contract price should be to guarantee under the ordinary condition of things what is looked upon as a fair compensation, probably in three cases out of four the contractor himself would look upon it as altogether too low a price. He could not see clearly himself how he could make as much money as this. You put this question to him : " If you could know as certainly as you can know anything that in managing twelve or fifteen men, and with the ordinary conditions of the work as they come along day after day, you could make five dollars a day for your own individual services, would not that be satisfactory ? " In the majority of cases the contractor will say : " Yes ; if I knew I could make five dollars a day, I should be perfectly satisfied." Well, then say to the contractor that you believe that he can do it ; that if after a fair trial you are satisfied that he has made a fair effort to do it, and if, after he has made that effort, you find that he could not make that amount, which you are perfectly willing that he should make, then it is an easy matter to readjust the price to his satisfaction ; or if he makes in excess of that amount, you can present to him the fact that he expressed himself as being satisfied if he could make five dollars a day, and there is an opportunity for readjustment in the other direction. At the same time it is the duty of the proprietor to do everything he can to supply that contractor with facilities for doing that work, so that he can keep the contract price down to what is a fair compensation for the workmen ; and in most cases the better facilities he provides for the workmen to do with, the better it is for himself. He reaps the benefit of it as well as the workmen. So that it is reduced to this point : How can we make it possible to make contracts for month after month or year after year without much if any change in the contract price ? If a rigid system of inspection is insisted upon and carried out, if the workman in his greediness or ambition to make more money slights his work, you always have it in your power to insist that the quality of the work shall be kept up to a certain standard ; or if you find that he can do better work than he is doing, instead of changing the price you can insist that the standard of the work shall be still more improved. So that it seems to me, in these days of apparent conflict between capital and labor, there is a way out of a great many troubles, and it is not only a business-like way, but it is a Christian way ; it brings into it some moral principles as well as other questions, and I believe that in that direction will be found the solution of this labor problem as between the manufacturer and the laborer.

Prof. J. B. Webb.—There is one point that has not been brought out. It is evident that a plan of this sort must tend to make each workman watch the others and feel anxious that every other man should do his full duty. It might even go so far in the case of a very poor workman as to make the rest exceedingly desirous to have him discharged; so much so, indeed, that they might even bring the desirability thereof in some way to the notice of the proprietor. I should like to know if in Mr. Towne's experience anything of that sort has occurred.

Mr. C. W. Nason.—I would like to say that I have tried in a limited way the gain-sharing system by giving the man under me in each department, the foreman, a certain interest in the year's business: making an annual contract, and giving each foreman an interest in the year's business. It appears to have worked satisfactorily. The shop I run chiefly on the basis of piece work, which after all appears to be a modified form of the gain-sharing system, and I found on piece work, if that is carefully estimated as to what a fair day's work is, that there is not very much reduction unless machinery is put in.

There are one or two questions I would like to ask. First, whether you have any idea what the percentage of cost of book-keeping amounts to when you have to go into detail, such as would be necessary in a shop of this sort. Secondly, whether in running a foundry, say on job-work, such as is coming in day after day, and will run say from $2\frac{1}{2}$ to 3 or 5 cents a pound,—whether in your opinion any system can be formed by which the gain-sharing device could be applied to it.

Mr. E. F. C. Davis.—I think that the success of these schemes depends more largely than anything else on the moral influence that the managers exercise over the men. I was with a friend a short time ago while the labor question was in a very delicate condition.

He wished to introduce the "piece work" system in the shop under his charge, but knew very well that the men would not allow it to be introduced without great trouble. So he told the men that he could not ask them to work piece work or by contract, but that in the machine shop he would allow a definite number of hours to do a certain job, and that of any time he saved from that he would get one-half the benefit. But the men did not seem to want to do that. He went to a very intelligent man and said, "That job you are on we have estimated to take ten hours ; we think it can be done in less than that ; if you can do it in less than that you can have the benefit of one-half of the time saved." He said, "I don't want to work that way." The other said, "If you do it and we pay you the one-half, you will not object to taking the money ?" The man simply smiled. He went on and did the work in less than ten hours. He took the half, and from that on there was no trouble. The whole thing went on afterwards on that principle. That is only one instance to show that success depends very largely on the moral influence which is brought to bear in dealing with the subject.

Another case I have in mind is that of a pretty large shop where piece work had been introduced. The men fought against it for some time. That is, they showed a cold disposition toward it. But it was brought about in this way : We told a man that we would set the price of each piece at about what we thought they could make it at, and if they could not make wages at that, we would allow them their wages, so that they would feel that we were not trying to grind them down ; but if they made more than 20 per cent. above their wages that their price would be reduced.

We found that that insured a fair profit to the concern, and it pleased the men ; and they are very well satisfied with it even to this day.

The piece work system does not always antagonize the men. These shops were part of a large concern which employed probably some thirty thousand men altogether, and only about seven hundred men were shop hands. The thirty thousand other men went out on a grand strike. In fact, all the employees of that company went on a strike, with the exception of the shop men, and they could not be induced to join the strike. They had fought against this piece work system up to within six months before that time, but they found in the meantime that it was working to their interest. The men understood that fact, and when the strike came about they refused to go out on strike. The fact that those shop men refused to go out had a very important bearing on the breaking up of the strike. They not only have stopped fighting against the system, but appreciate the benefits of it.

Mr. Parker.—I merely wish to mention one example in connection with this system of gain-sharing of which the paper speaks.

It is taken from my own experience. I had a contractor at work on certain class of machine work six years ago. The same contractor is working on the same class of work to-day. Six years ago the machinery and tools he had to do that work with were very much behind the age, and it was not possible to produce economically with them. He was making at that time a certain price per day. It became apparent that, to reduce the cost of production, it was necessary to give him better facilities and better tools. The subject was discussed with him, and he was asked the question, "If you can be supplied with machinery to enable you to produce that work at a reduction, and with the feeling all the time in your mind that you are not going to suffer any reduction of the net gain to yourself, will you submit to the reduction?" Such a man cannot help saying, "Certainly." It was tried and kept up more or less for four years, until the process was got down about as simple and direct as it could be. The result is, that the contractor to-day is making fifteen to eighteen per cent. larger net gain than he was six years ago, and the net contract cost to the proprietor is over forty per cent. below what it was six years ago.

The President.—If there are no further remarks I will close the discussion.

In the first place, the system is not complex or difficult. The only difficult part is the planning at its inception; and in most productive industries this is not a serious trouble and will certainly be somewhat helped by the description contained of the method in the paper, including the rules which are given at its close as in force at the works in question. After the method has been adapted to any particular business, its operation is an exceedingly simple thing.

To answer another question, the cost of the clerical work involved is comparatively trifling. I think I am right in saying that where the system is now in use some twenty-one contracts being in force affecting over three hundred men, the total increase of clerical work is much less than what would be accomplished by one ordinary clerk. I am quite within bounds in saying that one-half of the time of a good clerk would represent all the added work which the adoption of this system involves in that instance.

In answer to the question of Prof. Wood as to what happens when no profit is derived, I would call his attention to the fact that such a case cannot arise under this system. This is not profit sharing in which losses in business would disturb the relation, but simply an offer from the employer to give the employee a fraction of the *gain* or saving accomplished in the cost of work. If any saving is made, the employee gets his fraction of it; if no saving is made, he simply gets his wages. Mr. Parker's case of a loss by fire suggests simply to me the need that exists in all these matters of a clear, definite contract at the commencement. The feasibility of framing such a contract is illustrated by the foundry rules which cover three pages of this paper. They are brief; but I think they meet all the contingencies which would naturally arise.

The case of piece-work operations with prices for unfixed periods has been touched upon by several of the speakers, and that is a subject which I have referred to at our previous meetings, and which I have always looked upon as a blunder on the part of managers. If you give contract or piece work to a man and tell him that you reserve to yourself the right to reduce his rate at any time, you are simply taking away from him the stimulus to reduce the cost. Workmen know well enough that if they make large wages the employer will cut down their piece rate, and that in order to make larger earnings they must then work harder. The result is that where that system obtains, the workman gauges the point at which he thinks the employer will let him alone, and regulates his work so as not to produce more than that limit. In my experience I have found it exceedingly beneficial to make contract or piece rates for definite and usually for pretty long periods, always for twelve months, and in the case of older jobs, where the work is well understood, the rates are fixed for two, three and sometimes five years. The workman then has an inducement to do the best he can during that period, and at the end of it the reduction of cost has sometimes been surprisingly large.

In answer to Mr. Nason's question, in regard to a varied product, I would say, that in my case that difficulty is overcome by dividing the product into grades or classes, each of which has a graded pricing, and the foreman determining which grade the work belongs to at the time it is finished.

Want of faith on the part of the men in any system of this kind is a fact that has to be recognized and which is very apt to continue during the first year. As stated in the paper, the best possible argument wherewith to meet it is a cash dividend. In starting this system in the first instance, I encountered that difficulty very generally. The men were either indifferent or else hostile to it, believing that it was some scheme whereby the Company was to get more from them without paying for it. And in cases of that kind all you can do is to simply wait, and perhaps to reason a little with your more intelligent men. Induce them to use their influence to carry the thing into effect fairly, and at the end of the year pay them a dividend if it has been earned. Doubts and difficulties will disappear very promptly after the men have received the first dividend in cash.

Prof. Webb.—If each man watches the other, and each man notices that the eleventh man is not doing his share, would not they want to get rid of the eleventh man? In some cases, might they not even go so far as to make the proprietor aware of that fact?

The President.—I can say that the latter effect might not obtain in some cases, although it has not happened in my experience. The other effect is very marked, that the men are interested in the efficiency of the others about them, and that the men are all interested in economy in avoiding the waste of materials. The tendency of the system is unquestionably to raise the *morale* of the whole force, so that it acts beneficially in that respect as well as others.

THE PREMIUM PLAN
OF PAYING FOR LABOR

Frederick A. Halsey

CCCCXLIX.*

THE PREMIUM PLAN OF PAYING FOR LABOR.

BY F. A. HALSEY, SHERBROOKE, P. Q., CANADA.

(Member of the Society.)

THIS plan has been devised in order to overcome the objections inherent in the other plans in general use. It accomplishes this purpose without introducing corresponding objections of its own. Its merits are best shown by contrasting it with the other plans in common use, and it will be discussed with them in the following order :

I. The day's-work plan.
II. The piece-work plan.
III. The profit-sharing plan.
IV. The premium plan.

I. THE DAY'S-WORK PLAN.

Under this method the workman is paid for and in proportion to the time spent upon his work. The objections to the plan are well known. Analyzed to their final cause, they spring from the fact that any increase of effort by the workman redounds solely to the benefit of the employer, the workman having no share in the consequent increase of production. He has consequently no inducement to exert himself and does not exert himself. Under this system, especially in a manufacturing business, matters naturally settle down to an easy-going pace, in which the workmen have little interest in their work, and the employer pays extravagantly for his product.

II. THE PIECE-WORK PLAN.

Under this plan the workman is paid for and in proportion to the amount of work done. It is a natural attempt to overcome the objections to the day's-work plan. It has the appearance of being

---

* Presented at the Providence meeting (1891) of the American Society of Mechanical Engineers, and forming part of Volume XII. of the *Transactions*.

just and of being based upon correct principles. Nevertheless, extended inquiry has convinced the writer that it seldom works smoothly, and never produces the results which it should.

An employer who has become dissatisfied with the results of the day's-work plan, and decides to adopt piece work, usually reasons that work which is costing in wages, say one dollar per piece, could, with some extra effort, be produced on the existing scale of wages for about eighty cents; and desiring to give the workman some inducement offers him ninety cents per piece, thereby dividing the expected saving with him. The trouble begins at once. The workman does not believe that he can "make wages" at the rate offered, and objects. He is, however, finally induced or compelled to try it, and immediately proceeds to astonish himself and all others by increasing his output far beyond the expected 25%. His earnings increase with startling rapidity, *but the cost of the work remains where set, at ninety cents per piece,* and 'the employer soon finds that instead of a substantially equal division of the savings he is getting but little, and the workman practically all of it. He accordingly proceeds to cut the piece price, and the fatal defect of the system appears. This cut is in appearance and in fact an announcement to the workman that his earnings will not be allowed to exceed a certain amount, and that should he push them above that amount he will be met with another cut. Cutting the piece price is simply killing the goose that lays the golden egg. Nevertheless, the goose must be killed. Without it the employer will continue to pay extravagantly for his work; with it he will stifle the rising ambition of his men. The difficulties of the day's-work and piece-work plans are thus seen to be the exact antitheses of one another. Analyzed to their final cause, the difficulties with the piece-work plan spring from the fact that the piece price once set, any increase of effort by the workman redounds to *his own* benefit alone—the employer having no share in the consequent saving of time. To obtain a share he cuts the piece price, with the consequences stated. Under this system matters gradually settle down as before to an easy-going pace in which the workmen approach the limit of wages as nearly as they consider prudent. Their earnings are somewhat more and the cost of the work is somewhat less than under the day's-work plan, but there is no more spirit of progress than under the older method. The employer is constantly on the lookout for a chance to cut the piece prices, that being his only method of reducing cost; and the men are constantly on the lookout to defeat the employer's well understood plan, knowing, as they do, that any one who is so unwise or so unfortunate as to do an increased amount of work will be in effect punished for it by having his piece price cut and himself thereby compelled to work harder in the future for the old amount of income. The system makes the interests of the employer and employee antagonistic, and hence of concerted effort toward a progressive reduction of cost there is none. This I believe to be the usual and natural history of the piece-work plan. I know it to represent the situation in some of the foremost machine shops of the country. An additional objection to the plan grows out of the fact that it requires a knowledge and record of the cost of each piece of a complicated machine, and oftentimes of each operation on each piece. This limits its range of application to products which are produced in considerable quantities.

III. THE PROFIT-SHARING PLAN.

This plan was originally devised in the effort to avoid the objections to the two former plans. Under it, in addition to regular wages, the employees are offered a certain percentage of the final profits of the business. It thus divides the savings due to increased production between employer and employee, and at first sight appears to meet the difficulties of the plans thus far discussed; but, nevertheless, on analysis, will be found to be as defective as they, both in principle and application. The leading objections to the plan are the following:

First. The workmen are given a share in what they do not earn. Increased profits may arise from more systematic shop management, decreased expenses of the sales department, or many other causes with which the workmen have nothing to do. Anything given them from such sources becomes simply a gift, the result of which is wholly pernicious—in fact the entire system savors of patronage and paternalism.

Second. The workmen share, regardless of individual deserts. An active, energetic workman cannot have the same incentive to increased exertion under a system which divides the results of his efforts among a dozen lazy fellows at his side that he would have under one in which his earnings depend on himself alone; on the other hand, a lazy workman would naturally consider it much easier to take his portion of the earnings of his fellows than to exert himself and then divide the results with all the others of the force.

Third. The promised rewards are remote. The incentive cannot be as great under a system which computes and divides the savings once or twice a year as under one which pays out the extra earnings week by week.

Fourth. The plan makes no provision for bad years. We hear much of profit sharing, but nothing of loss sharing. And yet the workman cannot expect to share the profits while others assume the losses ; and, *per contra,* those who assume the risk of loss cannot be expected to share the profits with those who have nothing at stake.

Fifth. The workmen have no means of knowing if the agreement is carried out. With their exaggerated ideas of the profits of business, the results must be in many cases disappointingly small, and they will doubt the honesty of the division. What is to be done in such a case? Invite the workmen to appoint a committee to examine the books, and report? Most employers will demur at this, and yet without it the employees can have no assurance of good faith ; and were it done, what good could result? How many workmen's committees are there who are sufficiently versed in modern accounts to form any idea of the proceeds of the year's business from an examination of the books? In this light the profit-sharing plan is seen to be an agreement between two parties, the first of whom has every temptation and opportunity to cheat the second, while the second has no means of knowing if he has been cheated, and no redress in any case. In the present state of human nature this cannot be expected to be satisfactory to the second party. The fact that the plan has worked with apparent success in some instances and for considerable periods of time proves nothing. The most disastrous boiler explosions and bridge failures have been preceded by long periods of apparent safety. Even the Conemaugh dam held water for many years. It is a truism that the most rickety and unsafe devices often serve their purpose for long periods. At the beginning the workmen look on the amount received at the annual division as a bonus, and anything is better than nothing ; but later on they will look on it as theirs by right of having earned it, and the above situation is certain to arise. The fact is, that the profit-sharing plan is wrong in principle, and cannot be in any large sense a solution of the wages problem.

IV. THE PREMIUM PLAN.

Taking up now the subject proper of this paper, it aims at a division of the savings due to increased production between the employer and employee, but by a direct method instead of the circuitous one of the profit-sharing plan. The plan assumes two slightly different forms, according to the nature of the work; one form being suited to work produced in such quantities as to be reducible to a strictly manufacturing basis, and the other form to the more limited production of average practice. In both forms the essential principle is the same, as follows: The time required to do a given piece of work is determined from previous experience, and the workman, in addition to his usual daily wages, is offered a premium for every hour by which he reduces that time on future work, the amount of the premium being less than his rate of wages. Making the hourly premium less than the hourly wages is the foundation stone on which rest all the merits of the system, since by it if an hour is saved on a given product the cost of the work is less and the earnings of the workman are greater than if the hour is not saved, the workman being in effect paid for saving time. Assume a case in detail: Under the old plan a piece of work requires ten hours for its production, and the wages paid is thirty cents per hour. Under the new plan a premium of ten cents is offered the workman for each hour which he saves over the ten previously required. If the time be reduced successively to five hours the results will be as follows:

1	2	3	4	5
Time consumed.	Wages per piece.	Premium.	Total cost of work = col. 2 + col. 3.	Workman's earnings per hour = col. 4 + col. 1.
Hours.	$	$	$	$
10	3.00	0	3.00	.30
9	2.70	.10	2.80	.311
8	2.40	.20	2.60	.325
7	2.10	.30	2.40	.343
6	1.80	.40	2.20	.366
5	1.50	.50	2.00	.40

This table illustrates the manner in which the cost of the work diminishes and the workman's earnings increase together until, to cite the extreme case of the last line, if the output be doubled, the wages paid per piece will be reduced 33⅓%, but the workman's earnings per hour will be increased 33⅓%. Were the premium less than ten cents per hour, the reduction in cost for each hour saved would be greater, and the workman's earnings less. On the other hand, the workman would have a smaller incentive, and the time would not be reduced so much. The output would be less, and the net result might be worse for both employer and employee. This raises the inevitable question: What should be the rate of the premium? Nothing but good sense and judgment can decide in any case. In certain classes of work an increase of production is accompanied with a proportionate increase of muscular exertion, and if the work is already laborious a liberal premium will be required to produce results. In other classes of work increased production requires only increased attention to speeds and feeds with an increase of manual dexterity and an avoidance of lost time. In such cases a more moderate premium will suffice. Any attempt, however, on the part of the employer to be greedy and squeeze the lemon too dry will defeat its own object, since if a trifling premium be offered, the workman will not consider it worth while to exert himself for so small a reward, and the expected increase of output will not take place. On the other hand, if the premium offered be too high, the employer will simply pay more than necessary for his work, though less than he has been paying. If the rate of premium is decided upon judiciously, it may and should be made permanent. No cutting down of the rate should ever be made unless, indeed, improved processes destroy the significance of the first time base. Every increase of earnings is necessarily accompanied by a corresponding decrease of cost, and if the premium be such as to give these a satisfactory relation, the workman may be assured that there will be no limit set to his earnings; that the greater they are the more satisfactory they will be to the employer. The importance of this cannot be too strongly insisted upon. If the premiums be cut the workmen will rightly understand it to mean, as under the piece-work plan, that their earnings are not to be permitted to pass a certain limit, and that too much exertion is unsafe. The very purpose of the plan is to avoid this by so dividing the savings between employer and employee as to remove the necessity for cutting the rate, and hence enable the workman's earnings to be limited only by his own ability and activity. The baneful feature of the piece-work

plan is thus completely obviated, and instead of periodical cuts
with their resulting ill-feeling, the premiums lead the workman
to greater and greater effort, resulting in a constant increase of
output, decrease of cost, and increase of earnings.

The broad-minded employer will not fail to recognize that his
own gain from the system comes largely from the increased production from a given plant, since not only does the system reduce
the wages cost of the piece of work in hand, but in so doing it
increases the capacity of the plant for other work to follow. The
advantages from this source are so great as to render unnecessary
any refined hair splitting as to the rate of the premium.

Such is the premium plan, and the writer confidently predicts
that the more it is studied the more perfect will appear its adaptation to the requirements of industrial enterprise and human
nature.   Surely, a system which increases output, decreases cost,
and increases workman's earnings simultaneously, without friction,
and by the silent force of its appeal to every man's desire for a
larger income, is worthy of attention. In addition to the commanding features noted it has others of lesser note. The transi-
tion to it from the day's-work plan is easy and natural. It does
not involve a reorganization of the system of bookkeeping, but
only an addition, and a small one, to the existing system. No opposition to it, organized or otherwise, is possible, since there is
nothing compulsory about it, and nothing tangible to oppose. It
is simply an offer to gratify one of the strongest passions of
human nature, and the difficulty often found in introducing piece
work cannot occur with this.

In carrying out the plan in connection with work which has
been reduced to a manufacturing basis, the writer finds the following form of time ticket convenient:

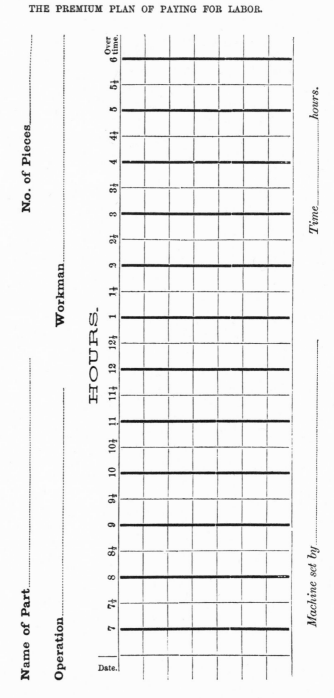

Time Ticket.

Name of Part

Operation

No. of Pieces

Workman

Machine set by

Time hours.

This ticket is issued by the foreman, the blanks at the top being filled up by him. If desired as a check he punches a hole on the line, indicating the hour when the work is given out, repeating the same when the work and ticket are returned. The record of the time is kept by drawing a line between the various hour marks, an operation which the most illiterate can perform.* The ticket provides for several days' work, and is not returned until the work is completed, when it contains the record of the entire job.† On the back of the ticket is printed the following:

" According to previous experience this work should require ... hours. If completed in less time than that a premium of ... cents will be paid for each hour saved."

When the ticket is returned, a comparison of the back with the front shows the premium earned. This is entered opposite the workman's name, in a book kept for the purpose, which is a companion to the usual time book or pay roll. On pay day the accrued premiums are paid to each workman along with the regular wages. The cost book is written up from the ticket in the usual way, except that as the ticket usually contains the record of several days' work, the labor of keeping the cost book is much abridged.

On work which, while produced as a regular product, is still not produced in sufficient quantity to justify recording the cost of each part, the premium offer is made to the group of men who carry out the work. The proposition is made as a posted notice, or otherwise in the following form:

" According to previous experience this work should require ... hours. If completed in less time than that a premium of ... cents per hour saved will be divided among those working on the machine, division to be in proportion to time spent on the work."

In this form the system loses the advantage of dealing directly with the individual, and the second objection to the profit-sharing plan is introduced, though in a modified degree, as a small group

---

* Attention was called to this form of time ticket by Professor Hutton in Vol. IX. of the *Transactions*, page 386.

† This rule holds, even when the job after being partly finished is interrupted by something more pressing. In such a case the ticket is taken up by the foreman in order to insure that the entries have been made for the completed work. He issues the ticket again when the work is resumed, and when all is completed this ticket goes to the office, where a single entry in the cost book records what, under the usual method, might require a half dozen or even more entries.

of men is dealt with instead of the entire force. The remaining objections to the profit-sharing plan are not introduced, and on such work the plan proposed is distinctly superior, though lacking theoretical perfection. The piece-work plan does not apply to work of this kind, and hence there can be no comparison between it and the plan under discussion.

On contract work undertaken for the first time the method is the same, except that the premium is based on the *estimated* time for the execution of the work.

The system is thus applicable to all classes of machine-shop work except "jobbing" or work done by the hour, and there is no very vociferous demand from the shops for a method of reducing the time on that class of work.

The writer believes that, judiciously administered, the plan proposed will produce a larger output and cheaper work, and at the same time pay higher wages than any other whatsoever.

DISCUSSION.

Mr. John T. Hawkins.—In this paper we have still another attempt to protect—to be plain—unfair workers and employers against encroachments upon each other's rights. It is of a piece with about all former attempts to substitute for the proper spirit of fair dealing between man and man in the two capacities, something which shall force both to observe what the whole history of this question shows cannot be so controlled.

If men would deal justly and fairly with one another in this matter, it is self-evident that the day's-work, or better, the hour's-work plan, is the ideal one ; but human cupidity on both sides interferes with its proper working, and the only remedy, in the writer's opinion, is to be found in some system of educating employers and workmen alike up to the fact that their common interests lie solely in each doing to the other what he would have the other do to him. But with such an observance of the golden rule would come the millennium ; and there is no very imminent prospect of great possibilities in this direction; nor will there be more than is brought about by the gradual but sure development of the race to higher ethical planes, unless some organized effort is made to school both sides up toward this ideal.

The writer fails to see in the proposed plan any surer escape from the evils of the time in the relations of employer and work-

man, than in the older ones which the author of the paper
mentions. In point of fact, it is far below the piece-work
plan, which has shown itself to be the only ameliorating system where practicable.

The author assumes a case in detail, and also assumes it possible in this case, to reduce the time required to produce a
given price of work by 50%. If we apply this to an average
manufacture, in which the labor constitutes one-half and material and expenses the other half of the total cost, with 10% profit
to the employer to make up his selling price, we have the unexistable conditions that the employer will thereafter realize
tabout 25% profit and the workman obtain 33% advance of wages
On its face this looks very well and would seem to deal quite·
fairly between the two; but the true state of the case is that
no manufacturer has any right to such a profit, and if the outside world would stand it, a much larger part of the saving
should accrue to the workman, whose labor produces the given
article ; this is of course providing we are prepared to condone in
the workman the fact that he was capable by a fair day's work
of doing double what he actually performed under an agreed
day's wages.

But there are others deeply interested in such a result
What of the consumer? He would say that these people were
getting rich at his expense and altogether too rapidly, that both
were in a fair way to become those terrors of the times, " robber
barons ; " and he looks about him for means of putting a little
of this undue enrichment, of this—as he would probably term
it—monopolistic combination of workman and employer, into
his own pocket ; then, appealing to the cupidity common to employer and employee, and taking counsel of his own, he proceeds to procure the starting up of rival concerns, who will be
satisfied with more legitimately low profits, and who would
obtain workmen at lower pay than that gotten by the workmen
in the aforesaid combination, and thus the initial wages rate
upon which 10 cents for each tenth of the time saved is ad-
vanced on the rate of premium, and the 25% profit of the manufacturer both succumb to the inexorable laws of trade and manufacture.

The author, in discussing the piece-work system, shows that
when the workman has " astonished himself and all others by
increasing his output far beyond the expected 25%," and " his

earnings increase with startling rapidity," " while the cost of the work remains the same," and says that under these conditions the employer, in cutting the prices, practically announces to the workman that " his earnings will not be allowed to exceed a certain amount," concludes that this cutting amounts to "killing the goose which lays the golden egg." Nevertheless this goose must be killed in any event. If the employer doesn't kill it, the consumer, through his competitors, will not only kill it, but him. The fact is that no such golden eggs are to be had in industrial pursuits, and it would be most unrighteous that they should.

As the writer has had occasion to contend in a previous discussion of this subject : If a workman at piece work succeeded in producing a piece of work in one-half the length of time he previously employed himself upon at day wages, there is no escape from the fact that, when working by the day he was not only robbing his employer, but the consumer of his product as well ; and it is to the credit of the piece-work system that it furnishes the means of discovering such a state of things.

The piece-work system, in the writer's opinion, furnishes the only relief from the unsatisfactory relations between employer and workman which so largely obtain under the day's wages plan ; while the older and still prevalent plan of paying a given sum for a given time, with a *quid pro quo* rendered, is that which will continue to prevail and improve—as it, of all the proposed systems only, is capable of improvement—as men themselves improve. It does not lie either in profit sharing or premium paying to ameliorate the regrettable features of this older plan, nor can any such amelioration come from any system which overlooks the iron laws of supply and demand.

In all the systems proposed, and in the newer more than in the original day-wages plan, human rapacity or cupidity defeats itself and with it the most promising of these new systems, whether it exists in the workman or employer or both; and when workmen learn that their interests lie in doing the best they can for an agreed compensation by the day or hour, and the employer similarly is persuaded that his success in the long run depends upon his paying the best wages that the market for his product will permit, commensurate with a fair profit to himself; paying always the highest wages to the best and most efficient workman, as a proper and legitimate incentive to increased effort on his part, we will have as nearly the ideal conditions as are possible in any industrial system.

Mr. E. F. C. Davis.—I have known several instances where the bonus plan was adopted, by which a certain amount of time was arrived at as being customary for certain work, and then cards were given out stating that half of the time saved would revert to the mechanic and half to the shop; and that established what might be considered a minimum amount of time which each job would be likely to require with the appliances then in hand. Those shops which are doing this have arrived at what may be considered fair piece-work prices, and, after using the premium plan a little while, have dropped it as being too cumbersome, and come down to the simple piece-work plan. But by starting out with the bonus plan first, they avoided the necessity of such extensive cutting and have gotten at fair piece-work prices by the bonus system, which was too cumbersome to keep up; but I have never known anybody who carried out Mr. Halsey's plan for any great length of time.

Mr. William O. Webber.—I think Mr. Davis has rather hit the nail on the head. Success in using the piece-work system results largely from making your prices right in the first place, and I think that can be easily done by a manager who thoroughly understands his business. On the other hand, I think that Mr. Hawkins has given one of the strongest points about the whole wage problem, and that is the willingness between both the employer and the employee to be absolutely fair with each other. We have found in the Erie City Iron Works, at Erie, Pennsylvania, that treating our men in that way has resulted not only to their advantage, but to ours. We have even had men come to us and say that the piece-work price for a certain piece of work was too much, comparing it with similar pieces of a different size. Now, we take that as a pointer, and if we find that, as in many cases, the prices seem high for a certain piece, we do not see anything unfair or unbusiness-like in going to the workman who is doing that work and suggesting a revision of those prices. Sometimes they can be revised with good reason. We recently had a workman in our works come and say this. We were paying him a certain price for planing cylinders. He said if we would give him a more modern planer, he would plane those pieces for 20% less. That was certainly a fair proposition on his part, and we immediately took it up. I think that the piece work system is the only one which will ever be successful in any way, and to make it a success, there must be a complete fairness between the employer and the employee, and the making of prices right in the first place, which any man who understands the business ought to know how to do.

Mr. William Kent.—I regret that Mr. Halsey has not given us actual data in his paper. I regret still more that Mr. Hawkins has presented an argument which is altogether *a priori* without any facts, except those drawn from experience with other systems than the premium system. Mr. Halsey some three or four years ago proposed to me this premium plan, and I fortunately was then in a position to put it in practice at once, and it has been in use in the shops of the Springer Torsion Balance Company now for three years, with satisfaction to both employer and employed. I heartily endorse the plan as admirable in every respect. It has given no trouble at all. I may admit with one of the other speakers that this plan may result finally in the piece-work plan pure and simple. Whenever experience has gone so far that you cannot improve the method of manufacture, and the workman has got into a rut, then the amount which he gets under the premium plan will be a certain amount per piece. You might just as well in that case pay him by the piece; but as long as there is any chance of improvement, and men have not reached the utmost limit of their skill or inventive powers, so long will the premium plan be a good incentive to the workmen. In practice under the working of this premium plan, we have perhaps a small piece of machine work to do, and we have no previous experience in making it, but we put a boy to work upon it, and find that by his ordinary skill in attending a machine, doing as he is told, he turns out say 100 pieces in a day. We tell him that there may be some quicker way of doing that work if he can find it out, and we tell him we will give him a quarter of a cent premium upon every piece he makes over 100 a day. Now, we have had the number of pieces turned out jump up to three hundred a day, and that simply by some little knack that the boy discovered, which he was under no obligation to discover, and which he had no incentive (except the premium) to discover; he was not cheating his employer by not inventing or discovering that method before, but when we gave him an incentive to try and discover something, why, he went to work and he succeeded and added 50% to his wages. This is an actual case, and not a hypothetical one. So I close as I began, by saying that I heartily endorse Mr. Halsey's plan, and I hope that gentlemen will not condemn the plan unheard, or until they have more data as to its actual working.

Mr. Frank H. Ball.—I am very glad indeed to hear what Mr. Kent has said on this subject. I recall—and I presume other members here recall—a paper entitled *"Gain-Sharing,"* that was read at the Erie meeting by our ex-president, Mr. Towne, describing a method very similar to the one which Mr. Halsey proposes. The difference between the two plans is simply this: In the plan of gain-sharing which Mr. Towne described, the business was divided into departments, and the men in each of these departments were given a share in whatever they would save over certain fixed prices. For instance, in a foundry they found that it cost a certain amount per ton for labor, and his plan was to divide with the men what they would save over this fixed cost. Mr. Halsey goes one step further and brings it down to the men individually. The argument which Mr. Towne made for his method as against the profit-sharing plan, was substantially the same as Mr. Halsey's argument, and he gave us to understand that the results were very satisfactory. Mr. Halsey proposes to deal directly with each man, and I think the idea is an excellent one. It seems to me that it has advantages over any other system that has been proposed. If any system other than day wages will work well, it seems to me this system will.

Mr. H. H. Suplee.—The gain-sharing plan has been in use at the works of the Yale & Towne Manufacturing Company, Stamford, and both parties are thoroughly satisfied with its operation. In discussion of this paper with Mr. Towne—and as I think he would have discussed it himself if he were present—he at once noticed the similarity of the method as being the gain-sharing method reduced to a smaller difference of subdivision—the same in principle, but only different in application.

Mr. Henry L. Gantt.—I think Mr. Kent's remarks are subject to another interpretation. If that boy using the same tools could by a little knack increase the product 300%, it seems to me that either the foreman was careless in giving him directions, or was lacking in knowledge; at all events, something was wrong to start with, and the problem resolves itself into the original question: What is a day's work?

Mr. Thos. R. Almond.—I wish to call to the attention of the members something that was stated soon after Mr. Towne's paper at one of the meetings in New York. A gentleman from Altoona stated a case which came under his immediate observation. There were two men who were requested to do their work by the piece, and during the three or four days that they were doing the work by the piece one of them went to the foreman and said, "I cannot make day pay this way," while the other man said, "I am making twice as much as I was by the day." Now, here was a case that you could not account for in any way excepting as stated by the foreman in the answer he made to the man: "The trouble is not between yourself and me; you must go to the Creator."

Mr. Hawkins.—I am prepared to admit the *a priori* character of the discussion that I presented (and I wrote it very hastily and with a view of simply eliciting discussion); at the same time, while the arguments of Mr. Kent and Mr. Suplee seem to be conclusive, from the fact that up to the present time the two systems adopted by the Springer Balance Company and the Yale & Towne Company "have been successful," they give us no measure of this supposed success, and I contend that the time is entirely too short within which they have been put into practice to settle anything in the question. The time will come with both those concerns when they will be ready to drop their new plans, or it will revert practically into the piece-work or day-work system, if it is one of those kinds of manufacture in which the piece-work plan is practicable. Unfortunately, in the machine business it is not practicable in many places. While I have no data, I venture to say that if data could be obtained from piece-work establishments, the working of that system as against the profit-sharing or the premium-paying plan would be shown to have been very much more successful. I can point to an establishment as long ago as from 1850 to 1860 where they established the piece-work system and expected to carry it out thoroughly in all departments, but they have practically dropped even this plan except in those particular special parts of the machine to which it could be most practically applied. It requires a long time to settle this question or any of these new ideas in connection with labor, and I venture to say that they will all finally come back to that one idea: that they must learn to treat one another right.

Mr. R. Van A. Norris.—This seems to be very much like the Pennsylvania Railroad's method of paying the engineers and firemen on their line a premium on coal saved. They allow a certain quantity of coal for the run, and then they pay a premium on all the coal that is saved. A plan resulting very similarly was in use in one of the copper mines in Michigan some years ago, where the mining was found to be very expensive and the powder bill was extremely high. The amount of powder used per cubic fathom of rock by each miner was posted on a bulletin board each month and a prize given to the man using the least. That resulted in a reduction of about one-third in the powder bill, and, as all work was done by contract, the result was a reduction of the contract prices and an increase in the amount of money made by the men.

Mr. E. F. C. Davis.—I think most of the objections raised against piece work are by people who have never had a good opportunity to observe how it works. It is very automatic and self-regulating in its workings. If one man is making too much on a job, and, by any particular appliance is making very much more than his employer thinks he ought to make, there are ten chances to one that somebody else in the shop will notice the money he is making and will come forward and make a bid to get that work at what he considers a fair profit for himself. So that the thing works all the time to the benefit of both parties. Whenever any new appliance is put to work, particularly by the foreman or the employer, no reasonable mechanic ever objects to having his prices changed in proportion. I think that the fact of the matter is that both the premium plan and the piece-work plan come down to very much the same thing. So far as my experience has gone, I think that people who have tried the premium plan have generally abandoned it and adopted the piece-work plan, as being a simpler way of getting about the same thing. The piece-work plan makes a little less bookkeeping.

Mr. James McBride.—The remarks this evening have proceeded entirely upon skilled labor. I want to make a few remarks about unskilled labor. The New York Dye Wood Extract and Chemical Company, of which I am superintendent, employs very largely unskilled labor. About two years ago the firm decided that they would set aside a portion of the earnings of the concern each year, to be divided among their employees

—not committing themselves in any way to their employees, but simply giving to them a certain amount of money, in January each year, when the laboring man needs it more than at any other season, all in a lump sum. That plan was adopted two years ago. The result, while not altogether satisfactory, has been a great improvement to the old system of simply paying them day's wages. We find among the skilled mechanics that those who can reason to a conclusion are very much in favor of it. Among the unskilled laborers, while a good many of them do not exactly comprehend it, they think a good deal of it, so much so that when they get a man in among them who was born tired they make it so hot for him that he is glad to get out. Our pay roll has decreased in some departments very materially from the fact that a good man refuses to work alongside of a poor man. I am in favor of some method by which a portion of the earnings can be divided among the employees. I do not know what is the best plan. We adopted this plan, as we thought it the best for our purposes, and so far as we have gone with it we are satisfied it has been an improvement. This disturbed condition of labor points to the conclusion that manufacturers in the future, in order to pacify their workmen and keep them quiet, will have to devise some means by which the workman can become a sharer in some way with his employer.

Prof. G. I. Alden.—Will the gentleman be willing to state what sum unskilled labor received, and what sum skilled labor received of this division of profit each year?

Mr. McBride.—The first year we paid the common laborers 5% upon the amount of money which they had received during the year, and we made it obligatory that the men should be prompt at their work; if they lost twenty days in the year, this per cent. was either kept from them, or it was reduced. We gave the skilled laborers 10% upon the amount which they had received during the year, and those men higher up received a little more. The first year every man received a percentage, but the second year we were obliged to make a discrimination, and those who were tardy in arriving at their work, instead of getting 5% got only 2½%, and the skilled men got 5% instead of 10%. The result of this discrimination has been that those men who have been docked have since been very regular in attendance; they have become the laughing-stock, as it were, of their fellow workmen, and they have tried to make a better record.

Mr. William H. Weightman.—I think that we might strike at the employers on this question. They are as ambitious for a profit as the employees. My dealings have been more with those operating shops, and I have found that I can save 50% by calling for contract prices, over what it would cost by arranging to pay "the actual cost" with a certain percentage of profit. I had the same party do two similar pieces of work. The first one he did by contract, and he admitted that he made 30% profit. Some six months after that I had a similar machine made, where there was a possibility of having to alter it, and, sooner than have any trouble in regard to these alterations after the contract was made, I told the party to keep track of the time and allow his own profit afterward. This one cost us three times as much as the other, in spite of the fact that we found there was no necessity for the alteration. So that of the two machines, one cost $80, the other cost $150; and while in the first instance he stated (he had forgotten the admission he had made) that he had made 30% at $80, in the other he stated that he made the exact amount that the 30% on $80 was. Thus while the employer and employee can hardly trust each other, sometimes the employer is a little doubtful himself and "the golden rule," a factor all around.

Mr. Hawkins.—In 1877 I took charge of a machinery establishment in the city of Brooklyn, and carried out the old plan. I did not know a single one of the workmen in the whole concern, but I called them all together and I talked to them just as an employer or superintendent should talk to a number of men, expecting them to do the best they could. I gave them to understand that if they did the best they could, due consideration would be given them, and reward to those who did the best in the way of wages; and a dismissal or reduction of pay of those who did the worst. In the course of two or three weeks I found it necessary to discharge half a dozen men, from the fact that I could of my own observation see that the work which they were doing was being "nursed." I discharged them as examples, and I found my action resulted in great improvement on the part of the rest of the men. I also took the other course and raised the wages of the men who were doing the best, and that made a still greater improvement. I carried that system through in that shop so long as the shop was carried on, and I think with a great deal of success; and I will place this success against that of Mr. Kent and Mr. Suplee, and I venture to say that if I were to start a shop to-morrow, I would adopt that course, keeping in proper touch with the men, and I would undersell every one of you who pay these premiums or adopt these other methods. (Laughter and applause.)

Having undersold you, the law of supply and demand steps in and forces you to modify or abandon your scheme in self-defence.

The great trouble with all these proposed systems is, that they only partially, if at all, discriminate between a man's ability and his willingness to do. The old system, properly adminis-tered, enables an employer to reward superior ability, with as good a means of discriminating against idleness or unwilling-ness; in which, of course, the employer is called upon to act fairly. The latter rewards a man in proportion to his ability, while the former too largely offers incentives merely to perform what was the man's obvious duty in any case. "Capital and labor could get on well enough together if there were not so many men trying to get capital without labor."

Mr. Daniel Ashworth.—I have listened very attentively to these remarks. The difficulty with so many fine-spun theories and Utopian ideas such as we have heard, is, that they are trying to get rid of one important factor, and that is the force of circum-stances from the commercial side. Mr. Hawkins touched upon a very important point, when he spoke about carrying out a cer-tain scheme to undersell his competitors. Now, mark you, this is one of the turning points. I know it from teachings of expe-rience among many branches of industry in the United States. Systems have been developed upon this question, upon which a manufacturing concern would step forward in the market by some process of distribution of the pay, in the shape of pre-miums and piece work, and the gentlemen on the other side would immediately figure it out how much cheaper they could sell these goods, and eventually they would invent some plan worse than before, because these competitors would be stirred up. There is the weak point. Cupidity dominates trade, and it is a constant attempt of one to over-reach the other. There is the figuring in the office very elaborately, and it is presented as an ultimatum to the employees, "that we propose to carry out this system," and it is carried out. As has been repeatedly said, it is just like the old story of the naval distribution of prize

money : you sift it on a ladder, and that which remains on the
rungs is for the men, and that which falls through is for the
officers.

I can point you to industries in the Ohio Valley, which for the
last twenty years have had a species of competition beyond a
parallel in the history of any industries in the world, and they
have been going right along. They have been indulging in
deception upon the great mass of their intelligent employees ;
they said there was no money in the business at all, that ruin
was staring them in the face, and yet those establishments have
been increased from one to four furnaces, and they have
branched out in the different valleys where the natural fuel
would reach them. With all our boasted civilization, we ignore
the fact that these workmen are becoming more and more intelligent every day. When you will take the intelligent working
masses and say to them, "Send your representative to us whom
you see fit to appoint to discuss these questions," then you will
have a starting point, and then you will have the data which have
been so much talked about to-night. And right there I wish to
say, as has been said by Mr. Webber, start right. When, in
God's name, ever was the time that the manufacturer had the right
figure ? Why, he would change it in six months. (Laughter.)

I stand here to-night to champion the other side of this question, because I know I am in the minority, and yet I know I am
right. We might talk until the crack of doom, and it would be
one man trying to over-reach the others. Intelligent men, such
as our mechanics are, should be, and they are, able to agree
with their employers upon an equitable basis.

Mr. Thomas R. Almond.—A case has come under my notice
to-day which illustrates what Mr. Ashworth says. This morning
I went to see a prominent business man of this city, who said :
"I have never met you before, sir. I had an impression that
you were a tall, thin, dried-up kind of a fellow whom I didn't
wish to see ; your letters to me were so peculiar, your prices
were always so stiff, that I formed an opinion of you that was far
from pleasant ; but, sir, I have learned to like your way of doing
business." And he added : "It is because we are all cutting
each other's throats, and trying to get each other's business that
our profits are 10% instead of 20% or 25%. If manufacturers
would all keep their prices so that we could rely upon them, we
could all maintain our prices." I take it, sir, that Mr. Ashworth

is decidedly correct. I said to my foreman four years ago: "I want you to make those goods and fix the prices yourself, and if these are satisfactory to me, I will not cut them as long as you work for me, and the market prices can be maintained." Since then I have increased his prices. I do not wish to laud my own actions in any sense, but I do believe Mr. Ashworth is correct every time when he says that the manufacturers and the dealers are more at fault than the workmen.

Mr. Weightman.—These experiences always result in four or five different concerns reducing their prices until they get to the point of cutting each other's throats, when they conclude to form a trust, binding each other to maintain a certain fixed price, by means of which they are safe against having their business ruined. Instances can readily be cited where concerns agree between themselves that they had been cutting the prices down too low on the strength of this style of competition, using employees as assistants in reducing the prices, until the concerns get in such a condition that they are not doing a safe business. They immediately conclude to form some plan by which they can control each other and keep from going down too low. A combination is formed, an agreement signed, and they work along smoothly with moderate safety. The employees still get their profits. The result is a slight advance, so that the companies as well as the employees are for the time being satisfied. If you can get employer and employee to trust each other and to believe in each other there will be some sort of an understanding in, though hardly a definite conclusion to, the labor problem.

Mr. Robert W. Hunt.—During a somewhat busy life I have been constantly thrown in contact with labor questions. In the great development of the Bessemer business we had constantly to meet new conditions, which caused all of us—both the men and the employers—considerable trouble. The product of last year would be a ridiculous amount to be satisfied with this year, and yet the same number of men would execute the work. This because inventive genius had devised, and much money had been expended in providing mechanical appliances which rendered it possible. These conditions had to be met in some way. Certainly under such conditions the men ought to be willing to work for less pay per ton, while still earning more per day. I do not wish to detain you by giving reminiscences, and will close by saying that in my judgment any step which is taken in good faith, looking toward the solution of this labor trouble, is worthy of respectful consideration; and before its trial it is dangerous for us to say that it will not work. If any gentleman at the head of an establishment is willing to make the experiment, in the name of humanity let us bid him God-speed. Let him try it, and then let him give us his results, and thus help his neighbor in his efforts to better humanity, and his own interests. Undoubtedly the foundation for the solution of these difficulties is the relations existing between the employer and the employee. If a manager is an able and fair man, he will succeed much more easily than if he is incompetent and unfair. Unfortunately there is another difficulty which has to be constantly encountered, and that is, that some man who does not work for you will come in and be supported by your men in his right to assert his authority to discuss with you your relations with your employees. I think that this is the most serious difficulty any fair-minded employer has to meet.

*Mr. Fred. A. Halsey.**—It is all very well to say, as Mr. Hawkins and others have done, that the true solution of the wages problem is for men to deal justly with one another, which in this connection means for the employee to exert himself to the utmost, and for the employer to pay as high wages as he can afford. Unfortunately, however, this is not in human nature; and, whatever the millennium may bring, the problem before the employers of to-day is to deal with human nature as it is. It is a truism that the average man will not work for others as for himself, and the average employer desires to get his product as cheaply as possible. This may seem culpable to Mr. Hawkins, but to the writer it seems natural, just, and proper. At all events it is inevitable, and it is the purpose of the premium plan to provide for, and make use of, these features of human nature by giving the employee an opportunity to work in a measure for himself, and by giving the employer the assurance of a more than proportionate increase of product from a given increase of wages.

Mr. Hawkins's objection that the plan involves the "unexistable" condition of a profit of 25%, and that the manufacturer has no right to such a profit, seems to me irrelevant. Such arguments do not prevail against facts, and while, of course, it is not to be

---

* Author's Closure.

expected that the system will produce a general increase of output of 100%,* it is nevertheless true that in individual operations that figure has often been exceeded, and that too when such foremanship talent as was available had not discovered anything wrong with previous records.

Mr. Hawkins's third objection, that rival concerns would spring up, and by avoiding the premiums, produce the work that much cheaper, is based upon the assumption that the premiums are a charge upon production, *i.e.*, that the same production can be had without as with them. This is the kernel of the question, and here I believe Mr. Hawkins to be wholly wrong. He here, as, indeed, all along, confounds plans based on the profit-sharing principle, viz.: the division of a percentage of the profits among the employees in the general faith that the promise of such division will buy their good will, and thereby lead them to increase their product, at least enough to make up the amount divided among them, *but which amount is to be divided whether the increase really takes place or not*, with the present system in which the premiums are paid only in case of actual increase. With the first system the increase must take place, or the cost of production is raised, but with the second system this is impossible. There could be no better place to try the question to a conclusion than such a shop as Mr. Hawkins proposes, where the day's-work method is employed in the most enlightened manner. Mr. Hawkins may find a few men (I have never found one) who will produce as much on the day's-wages method as when offered the inducement of the premium plan; but that is not, and never will be, the case with an entire force, and if a single man of the force is susceptible to such inducement the plan applied to him will cheapen the product. *If it does not reduce the cost there will be no premiums to pay.* The fact is, that the average employer, foreman, or workman who has seen machine tools operated only on the day's-work system, does not know what they are capable of producing; and to those who have seen them worked under systems analogous to the one proposed, to claim that as good results can be obtained under day's-work methods, seems absurd.

---

* The table on page 759 is given merely as an illustration to explain the working of the system. There is nothing about it, or in connection with it, to justify the implication that the last line of the table represents an average result to be expected from the system.

Turning now to Mr. Davis's remarks, I have no shadow of doubt that his workmen could, and to one possessing their con-fidence would, draw a very different picture from his as to the "automatic" feature of piece work. Mr. Davis seems to have succeeded in getting his men to compete with one another. Few have succeeded in this, the usual reduction in the piece prices being brought about by a direct cut by the employer. However the results are the same. Each workman knows that if he push his earnings above a more or less clearly defined limit, some other workman will underbid him, and he would be foolish indeed were he too active. When men know, as under piece work all do know, that their earnings will not be allowed to exceed a certain limit, it is idle to expect them to exert them-selves to pass that limit, and right here is the essential differ-ence between the piece-work plan and the one under discussion, which some seem unable to see. The piece-work plan neces-sarily sets such a limit, while the present one does not. As to the system furnishing a mere stepping stone to the piece-work plan, its case is exactly analogous to a mathematical limit. When improvement can go no further, the system may be turned into piece work ; but that, like a mathematical limit, is a condi-tion which we forever approach but can never reach.

As the system proposed has excited considerable interest I add a few practical hints to any who may feel disposed to give it a trial. The first of these is a caution against expecting the work-men to receive it with any enthusiasm ; on the contrary, they will in most cases look upon it as piece work in disguise, and that sys-tem is so excessively and justly unpopular, that they will at first regard the present plan with suspicion. A little patience on the part of the employer, and a little experience on the part of the employee, will correct this, as the workmen find that the pre-miums are not a myth.

It has been pointed out in the body of the paper, that the sys-tem enables an employer to deal liberally with his men. At the same time there are two directions which this liberality can take. One method—and the wrong one—is to take the best record obtainable as a base, and then offer a liberal premium for its reduction. No force can be composed entirely of "stars," and if the above plan is followed it will be but a question of a short time when an inferior man will be put upon that job, who will soon find that he cannot equal the base rate, and he will cease trying. At the same time, a really superior man on the same job might push his earnings so high, in consequence of the large premium, as to tempt the employer to the fatal step of cutting down the premium. To meet this condition, I have adopted the settled policy of being liberal with the time rate rather than the premium rate, thus giving all a chance, and keeping the premiums within satisfactory limits.

Whatever may be the final policy in this particular, the system should be inaugurated at least with moderate premiums, since if its experimental premiums are made too low, no one can object to their being raised, whereas, should they be too high, it is another matter to lower them. In this connection, the table on page 759 was intended solely as an illustration of the principle of the system. As a matter of fact, a premium rate such as is there given would be altogether too high for the ordinary run of light machine-shop work, while for other and more laborious work, it might be altogether too low. As a matter of fact, I have produced excellent results with premiums as low as three cents an hour.

Finally, it is but just to himself that the author should add that this method has been in no way suggested by Mr. Towne's excellent gain-sharing system. In point of fact, the present plan was clearly formulated before the publication of Mr. Towne's paper. Its publication has been deferred in order that it might first receive practical trial, and be presented with a corresponding measure of assurance. It has now been tried in three establishments, and in each case with results such as have been described.

A PIECE-RATE SYSTEM

Frederick W. Taylor

DCXLVII.*

A PIECE-RATE SYSTEM,

BEING

A STEP TOWARD PARTIAL SOLUTION OF THE LABOR PROBLEM.

BY FRED. W. TAYLOR, GERMANTOWN, PHILADELPHIA, PA.

(Member of the Society.)

INTRODUCTION.

THE ordinary piece-work system involves a permanent antagonism between employers and men, and a certainty of punishment for each workman who reaches a high rate of efficiency. The demoralizing effect of this system is most serious. Under it, even the best workmen are forced continually to act the part of hypocrites, to hold their own in the struggle against the encroachments of their employers.

The system introduced by the writer, however, is directly the opposite, both in theory and in its results. It makes each workman's interests the same as that of his employer, pays a premium for high efficiency, and soon convinces each man that it is for his permanent advantage to turn out each day the best quality and maximum quantity of work.

The writer has endeavored in the following pages to describe the system of management introduced by him in the works of the Midvale Steel Company, of Philadelphia, which has been employed by them during the past ten years with the most satisfactory results.

The system consists of three principal elements:

(1) An elementary rate-fixing department.

(2) The differential rate system of piece-work.

(3) What he believes to be the best method of managing men who work by the day.

Elementary rate-fixing differs from other methods of making

---

* Presented at the Detroit Meeting (June, 1895) of the American Society of Mechanical Engineers, and forming part of Volume XVI. of the *Transactions*.

piece-work prices in that a careful study is made of the time required to do each of the many elementary operations into which the manufacturing of an establishment may be analyzed or divided. These elementary operations are then classified, recorded, and indexed, and when a piece-work price is wanted for work, the job is first divided into its elementary operations, the time required to do each elementary operation is found from the records, and the total time for the job is summed up from these data. While this method seems complicated at the first glance, it is, in fact, far simpler and more effective than the old method of recording the time required to do whole jobs of work, and then, after looking over the records of similar jobs, guessing at the time required for any new piece of work.

The differential rate system of piece-work consists briefly in offering two different rates for the same job ; a high price per piece, in case the work is finished in the shortest possible time and in perfect condition, and a low price, if it takes a longer time to do the job, or if there are any imperfections in the work. (The high rate should be such that the workman can earn more per day than is usually paid in similar establishments.) This is directly the opposite of the ordinary plan of piece-work, in which the wages of the workmen are reduced when they increase their productivity.

The system by which the writer proposes managing the men who are on day-work consists in paying *men* and not *positions*. Each man's wages, as far as possible, are fixed according to the skill and energy with which he performs his work, and not according to the position which he fills. Every endeavor is made to stimulate each man's personal ambition. This involves keeping systematic and careful records of the performance of each man, as to his punctuality, attendance, integrity, rapidity, skill, and accuracy, and a readjustment from time to time of the wages paid him, in accordance with this record.

The advantages of this system of management are :

First. That the manufactures are produced cheaper under it, while at the same time the workmen earn higher wages than are usually paid.

Second. Since the rate-fixing is done from accurate knowledge instead of more or less by guess-work, the motive for holding back on work, or "soldiering," and endeavoring to deceive the employers as to the time required to do work, is entirely removed, and with it the greatest cause for hard feelings and war between the management and the men.

Third. Since the basis from which piece-work as well as day rates are fixed is that of exact observation, instead of being founded upon accident or deception, as is too frequently the case under ordinary systems, the men are treated with greater uniformity and justice, and respond by doing more and better work.

Fourth. It is for the common interest of both the management and the men to coöperate in every way, so as to turn out each day the maximum quantity and best quality of work.

Fifth. The system is rapid, while other systems are slow, in attaining the maximum productivity of each machine and man ; and when this maximum is once reached, it is automatically maintained by the differential rate.

Sixth. It automatically selects and attracts the best men for each class of work, and it develops many first-class men who would otherwise remain slow or inaccurate, while at the same time it discourages and sifts out men who are incurably lazy or inferior.

Finally. One of the chief advantages derived from the above effects of the system is, that it promotes a most friendly feeling between the men and their employers, and so renders labor unions and strikes unnecessary.

There has never been a strike under the differential rate system of piece-work, although it has been in operation for the past ten years in the steel business, which has been during this period more subject to strikes and labor troubles than almost any other industry.   In describing the above system of management, the writer has been obliged to refer to other piece-work methods, and to indicate briefly what he believes to be their shortcomings.

As but few will care to read the whole paper, the following index to its contents is given :

INDEX.

1. Capital demands fully twice the return for money placed
in manufacturing enterprises that it does for real estate or

transportation ventures. And this probably represents the difference in the risk between these classes of investments.

2. Among the risks of a manufacturing business, by far the greatest is that of bad management; and of the three managing departments, the commercial, the financiering, and the productive, the latter, in most cases, receives the least attention from those that have invested their money in the business, and contains the greatest elements of risk. This risk arises not so much from the evident mismanagement, which plainly discloses itself through occasional strikes and similar troubles, as from the daily more insidious and fatal failure on the part of the superintendents to secure anything even approaching the maximum work from their men and machines.

3. It is not unusual for the manager of a manufacturing business to go most minutely into every detail of the buying and selling and financiering, and arrange every element of these branches in the most systematic manner, and according to principles that have been carefully planned to insure the business against almost any contingency which may arise, while the manufacturing is turned over to a superintendent or foreman, with little or no restrictions as to the principles and methods which he is to pursue, either in the management of his men or the care of the company's plant.

4. Such managers belong distinctly to the old school of manufacturers; and among them are to be found, in spite of their lack of system, many of the best and most successful men of the country. They believe in men, not in methods, in the management of their shops; and what they would call system in the office and sales departments, would be called red tape by them in the factory. Through their keen insight and knowledge of character they are able to select and train good superintendents, who in turn secure good workmen; and frequently the business prospers under this system (or rather, lack of system) for a term of years.

5. The modern manufacturer, however, seeks not only to secure the best superintendents and workmen, but to surround each department of his manufacture with the most carefully woven network of system and method, which should render the business, for a considerable period, at least, independent of the loss of any one man, and frequently of any combination of men.

6. It is the lack of this system and method which, in the judg-

ment of the writer, constitutes the greatest risk in manufacturing; placing, as it frequently does, the success of the business at the hazard of the health or whims of a few employees.

7. Even after fully realizing the importance of adopting the best possible system and methods of management for securing a proper return from employees and as an insurance against strikes and the carelessness and laziness of men, there are difficulties in the problem of selecting methods of management which shall be adequate to the purpose, and yet be free from red tape, and inexpensive.

8. The literature on the subject is meagre, especially that which comes from men of practical experience and observation. And the problem is usually solved, after but little investigation, by the adoption of the system with which the managers are most familiar, or by taking a system which has worked well in similar lines of manufacture.

9. Now, among the methods of management in common use there is certainly a great choice; and before describing the "differential rate" system it is desirable to briefly consider the more important of the other methods.

10. The simplest of all systems is the "day-work" plan, in which the employees are divided into certain classes, and a standard rate of wages is paid to each class of men; the laborers all receiving one rate of pay, the machinists all another rate, and the engineers all another, etc. The men are paid according to the position which they fill, and not according to their individual character, energy, skill, and reliability.

11. The effect of this system is distinctly demoralizing and levelling; even the ambitious men soon conclude that since there is no profit to them in working hard, the best thing for them to do is to work just as little as they can and still keep their position. And under these conditions the invariable tendency is to drag them all down even below the level of the medium.

12. The proper and legitimate answer to this herding of men together into classes, regardless of personal character and performance, is the formation of the labor union, and the strike, either to increase the rate of pay and improve conditions of employment, or to resist the lowering of wages and other encroachments on the part of employers.

13. The necessity for the labor union, however, disappears when *men* are paid, and not *positions;* that is, when the em-

ployers take pains to study the character and performance of each of their employees and pay them accordingly, when accurate records are kept of each man's attendance, punctuality, the amount and quality of work done by him, and his attitude towards his employers and fellow-workmen.

As soon as the men recognize that they have free scope for the exercise of their proper ambition, that as they work harder and better their wages are from time to time increased, and that they are given a better class of work to do—when they recognize this, the best of them have no use for the labor union.

14. Every manufacturer must from necessity employ a certain amount of day-labor which cannot come under the piece-work system; and yet how few employers are willing to go to the trouble and expense of the slight organization necessary to handle their men in this way? How few of them realize that, by the employment of an extra clerk and foreman, and a simple system of labor returns, to record the performance and readjust the wages of their men, so as to stimulate their personal ambition, the output of a gang of twenty or thirty men can be readily doubled in many cases, and at a comparatively slight increase of wages per capita!

15. The clerk in the factory is the particular horror of the old-style manufacturer. He realizes the expense each time that he looks at him, and fails to see any adequate return; yet by the plan here described the clerk becomes one of the most valuable agents of the company.

16. If the plan of grading labor and recording each man's performance is so much superior to the old day-work method of handling men, why is it not all that is required? Because no foreman can watch and study all of his men all of the time, and because any system of laying out and apportioning work, and of returns and records, which is sufficiently elaborate to keep proper account of the performance of each workman, is more complicated than piece-work. It is evident that that system is the best which, in attaining the desired result, presents in the long run the course of least resistance.

17. The inherent and most serious defect of even the best managed day-work lies in the fact that there is nothing about the system that is self-sustaining. When once the men are working at a rapid pace, there is nothing but the constant, unremitting watchfulness and energy of the management to keep

them there; while with every form of piece-work each new rate that is fixed insures a given speed for another section of work, and to that extent relieves the foreman from worry.

18. From the best type of day-work to ordinary piece-work the step is a short one. With good day-work the various opera'ions of manufacturing should have been divided into small sections or jobs, in order to properly gauge the efficiency of the men; and the quickest time should have been recorded in which each operation has been performed. The change from paying by the hour to paying by the job is then readily accomplished.

19. The theory upon which the ordinary system of piece-work operates to the benefit of the manufacturer is exceedingly simple. Each workman, with a definite price for each job before him, contrives a way of doing it in a shorter time, either by working harder or by improving his method; and he thus makes a larger profit. After the job has been repeated a number of times at the more rapid rate, the manufacturer thinks that he should also begin to share in the gain, and therefore reduces the price of the job to a figure at which the workman, although working harder, earns, perhaps, but little more than he originally did when on day-work.

20. The actual working of the system, however, is far different. Even the most stupid man, after receiving two or three piece-work "cuts" as a reward for his having worked harder, resents this treatment and seeks a remedy for it in the future. Thus begins a war, generally an amicable war, but none the less a war, between the workmen and the management. The latter endeavors by every means to induce the workmen to increase the output, and the men gauge the rapidity with which they work, so as never to earn over a certain rate of wages, knowing that if they exceed this amount the piece-work price will surely be cut, sooner or later.

21. But the war is by no means restricted to piece-work. Every intelligent workman realizes the importance, to his own interest, of starting in on each new job as slowly as possible. There are few foremen or superintendents who have anything but a general idea as to how long it should take to do a piece of work that is new to them. Therefore, before fixing a piece-work price, they prefer to have the job done for the first time by the day. They watch the progress of the work as closely as their other duties will permit, and make up their minds how quickly

it can be done. It becomes the workman's interest then to go just as slowly as possible, and still convince his foreman that he is working well.

22. The extent to which, even in our largest and best-managed establishments, this plan of holding back on the work—"marking time," or "soldiering," as it is called—is carried on by the men, can scarcely be understood by one who has not worked among them. It is by no means uncommon for men to work at the rate of one-third, or even one-quarter, their maximum speed, and still preserve the appearance of working hard. And when a rate has once been fixed on such a false basis, it is easy for the men to nurse successfully "a soft snap" of this sort through a term of years, earning in the meanwhile just as much wages as they think they can without having the rate cut.

23. Thus arises a system of hypocrisy and deceit on the part of the men which is thoroughly demoralizing, and which has led many workmen to regard their employers as their natural enemies, to be opposed in whatever they want, believing that whatever is for the interest of the management must necessarily be to their detriment.

24. The effect of this system of piece-work on the character of the men is, in many cases, so serious as to make it doubtful whether, on the whole, well-managed day-work is not preferable.

25. There are several modifications of the ordinary method of piece-work which tend to lessen the evils of the system, but I know of none that can eradicate the fundamental causes for war, and enable the managers and the men to heartily coöperate in obtaining the maximum product from the establishment. It is the writer's opinion, however, that the differential rate system of piece-work, which will be described later, in most cases entirely harmonizes the interests of both parties.

26. One method of temporarily relieving the strain between workmen and employers consists in reducing the price paid for work, and at the same time guaranteeing the men against further reduction for a definite period. If this period be made sufficiently long, the men are tempted to let themselves out and earn as much money as they can, thus " spoiling " their own job by another " cut " in rates when the period has expired.

27. Perhaps the most successful modification of the ordinary system of piece-work is the " gain-sharing plan." This was invented by Mr. Henry R. Towne, in 1886, and has since been

extensively and successfully applied by him in the Yale & Towne Manufacturing Co., at Stamford, Conn. It was admirably described in a paper which he read before this Society in 1888. This system of paying men is, however, subject to the serious, and I think fatal, defect that it does not recognize the personal merit of each workman; the tendency being rather to herd men together and promote trades-unionism, than to develop each man's individuality.

28. A still further improvement of this method was made by Mr. F. A. Halsey, and described by him in a paper entitled "The Premium Plan of Paying for Labor," and presented to this Society in 1891. Mr. Halsey's plan allows free scope for each man's personal ambition, which Mr. Towne's does not.

29. Messrs. Towne and Halsey's plans consist briefly in recording the cost of each job as a starting-point at a certain time; then, if, through the effort of the workmen in the future, the job is done in a shorter time and at a lower cost, the gain is divided among the workmen and the employer in a definite ratio, the workmen receiving, say, one-half, and the employer one-half.

30. Under this plan, if the employer lives up to his promise, and the workman has confidence in his integrity, there is the proper basis for coöperation to secure sooner or later a large increase in the output of the establishment.

Yet there still remains the temptation for the workman to "soldier" or hold back while on day-work, which is the most difficult thing to overcome. And in this as well as in all the systems heretofore referred to, there is the common defect: that the starting-point from which the first rate is fixed is unequal and unjust. Some of the rates may have resulted from records obtained when a good man was working close to his maximum speed, while others are based on the performance of a medium man at one-third or one-quarter speed. From this follows a great inequality and injustice in the reward even of the same man when at work on different jobs. The result is far from a realization of the ideal condition in which the same return is uniformly received for a given expenditure of brains and energy. Other defects in the gain-sharing plan, and which are corrected by the differential rate system, are:

(1) That it is slow and irregular in its operation in reducing costs, being dependent upon the whims of the men working under it.

(2) That it fails to especially attract first-class men and discourage inferior men.

(3) That it does not automatically insure the maximum output of the establishment per man and machine.

31. Coöperation, or profit sharing, has entered the mind of every student of the subject as one of the possible and most attractive solutions of the problem ; and there have been certain instances, both in England and France, of at least a partial success of coöperative experiments.

So far as I know, however, these trials have been made either in small towns, remote from the manufacturing centres, or in industries which in many respects are not subject to ordinary manufacturing conditions.

32. Coöperative experiments have failed, and, I think, are generally destined to fail, for several reasons, the first and most important of which is, that no form of coöperation has yet been devised in which each individual is allowed free scope for his personal ambition. This always has been and will remain a more powerful incentive to exertion than a desire for the general welfare. The few misplaced drones, who do the loafing and share equally in the profits with the rest, under coöperation are sure to drag the better men down toward their level.

33. The second and almost equally strong reason for failure lies in the remoteness of the reward. The average workman (I don't say all men) cannot look forward to a profit which is six months or a year away. The nice time which they are sure to have to-day, if they take things easily, proves more attractive than hard work, with a possible reward to be shared with others six months later.

34. Other and formidable difficulties in the path of coöperation are, the equitable division of the profits, and the fact that, while workmen are always ready to share the profits, they are neither able nor willing to share the losses. Further than this, in many cases, it is neither right nor just that they should share either in the profits or the losses, since these may be due in great part to causes entirely beyond their influence or control, and to which they do not contribute.

35. When we recognize the real antagonism that exists between the interests of the men and their employers, under all of the systems of piece-work in common use ; and when we re-

member the apparently irreconcilable conflict implied in the fundamental and perfectly legitimate aims of the two : namely, on the part of the men :

THE UNIVERSAL DESIRE TO RECEIVE THE LARGEST POSSIBLE WAGES FOR THEIR TIME.

And on the part of the employers :

THE DESIRE TO RECEIVE THE LARGEST POSSIBLE RETURN FOR THE WAGES PAID.

What wonder that most of us arrive at the conclusion that no system of piece-work can be devised which shall enable the two to coöperate without antagonism, and to their mutual benefit ?

36. Yet it is the opinion of the writer, that even if a system has not already been found which harmonizes the interests of the two, still the basis for harmonious coöperation lies in the two following facts :

First. That the workmen in nearly * *every trade can and will materially increase their present output per day, providing they are assured of a permanent and larger return for their time than they have heretofore received.*

Second. That the employers can well afford to pay higher wages per piece even permanently, providing each man and machine in the establishment turns out a proportionately larger amount of work.

37. The truth of the latter statement arises from the well-recognized fact that, in most lines of manufacture, the indirect expenses equal or exceed the wages paid directly to the workmen, and that these expenses remain approximately constant, whether the output of the establishment is great or small.

From this it follows that it is always cheaper to pay higher wages to the workmen when the output is proportionately increased ; the diminution in the indirect portion of the cost per piece being greater than the increase in wages. Many manufacturers, in considering the cost of production, fail to realize the effect that the *volume of output has on the cost.* They lose sight of the fact that taxes, insurance, depreciation, rent, interest, sal-

---

* The writer's knowledge of the speed attained in the manufacture of textile goods is very limited. It is his opinion, however, that owing to the comparative uniformity of this class of work, and the enormous number of machines and men engaged on similar operations, the maximum output per man and machine is more nearly realized in this class of manufactures than in any other. If this is the case, the opportunity for improvement does not exist to the same extent here as in other trades. Some illustrations of the possible increase in the daily output of men and machines are given in paragraphs 78 to 82.

aries, office expenses, miscellaneous labor, sales expenses, and frequently the cost of power (which in the aggregate amount to as much as wages paid to workmen), remain about the same whether the output of the establishment is great or small.

38. In our endeavor to solve the piece-work problem by the application of the two fundamental facts above referred to, let us consider the obstacles in the path of harmonious coöperation, and suggest a method for their removal.

39. The most formidable obstacle is the lack of knowledge on the part of both the men and the management (but chiefly the latter) of the quickest time in which each piece of work can be done; or, briefly, the lack of accurate time-tables for the work of the place.

40. The remedy for this trouble lies in the establishment in every factory of a proper rate-fixing department; a department which shall have equal dignity and command equal respect with the engineering and managing departments, and which shall be organized and conducted in an equally scientific and practical manner.

41. The rate-fixing, as at present conducted, even in our best-managed establishments, is very similar to the mechanical engineering of fifty or sixty years ago. Mechanical engineering at that time consisted in imitating machines which were in more or less successful use, or in guessing at the dimensions and strength of the parts of a new machine; and as the parts broke down or gave out, in replacing them with stronger ones. Thus each new machine presented a problem almost independent of former designs, and one which could only be solved by months or years of practical experience and a series of break-downs.

Modern engineering, however, has become a study, not of individual machines, but of the resistance of materials, the fundamental principles of mechanics, and of the elements of design.

42. On the other hand, the ordinary rate-fixing (even the best of it), like the old-style engineering, is done by a foreman or superintendent, who, with the aid of a clerk, looks over the record of the time in which a whole job was done as nearly like the new one as can be found, and then guesses at the time required to do the new job. No attempt is made to analyze and time each of the classes of work, or elements of which a job is composed; although it is a far simpler task to resolve each job

into its elements, to make a careful study of the quickest time in which each of the elementary operations can be done, and then to properly classify, tabulate, and index this information, and use it when required for rate fixing, than it is to fix rates, with even an approximation to justice, under the common system of guessing.

43. In fact, it has never occurred to most superintendents that the work of their establishments consists of various combinations of elementary operations which can be timed in this way; and a suggestion that this is a practical way of dealing with the piece-work problem usually meets with derision, or, at the best, with the answer that "It might do for some simple business, but my work is entirely too complicated."

44. Yet this elementary system of fixing rates has been in successful operation for the past ten years, on work complicated in its nature, and covering almost as wide a range of variety as any manufacturing that the writer knows of. In 1883, while foreman of the machine shop of the Midvale Steel Company of Philadelphia, it occurred to the writer that it was simpler to time each of the elements of the various kinds of work done in the place, and then find the quickest time in which each job could be done, by summing up the total times of its component parts, than it was to search through the records of former jobs, and guess at the proper price. After practising this method of rate-fixing himself for about a year, as well as circumstances would permit, it became evident that the system was a success. The writer then established the rate-fixing department, which has given out piece-work prices in the place ever since.

45. This department far more than paid for itself from the very start; but it was several years before the full benefits of the system were felt, owing to the fact that the best methods of making and recording time observations of work done by the men, as well as of determining the maximum capacity of each of the machines in the place, and of making working-tables and time-tables, were not at first adopted.

46. Before the best results were finally attained in the case of work done by metal-cutting tools, such as lathes, planers, boring mills, etc., a long and expensive series of experiments was made, to determine, formulate, and finally practically apply to each machine the law governing the proper cutting speed of tools; namely, the effect on the cutting speed of altering any

one of the following variables : the shape of the tool (*i.e.*, lip angle, clearance angle, and the line of the cutting edge), the duration of the cut, the quality or hardness of the metal being cut, the depth of the cut, and the thickness of the feed or shaving.

47. It is the writer's opinion that a more complicated and difficult piece of rate-fixing could not be found than that of determining the proper price for doing all kinds of machine work on miscellaneous steel and iron castings and forgings, which vary in their chemical composition from the softest iron to the hardest tool steel. Yet this problem was solved through the rate-fixing department and the "differential rate." with the final result of completely harmonizing the men and the management, in place of the constant war that existed under the old system. At the same time the quality of the work was improved, and the output of the machinery and the men was doubled, and, in many cases, trebled. At the start there was naturally great opposition to the rate-fixing department, particularly to the man who was taking time observations of the various elements of the work; but when the men found that rates were fixed without regard to the records of the quickest time in which they had actually done each job, and that the knowledge of the department was more accurate than their own, the motive for hanging back or "soldiering" on this work ceased, and with it the greatest cause for antagonism and war between the men and the management.

48. As an illustration of the great variety of work to which elementary rate-fixing has already been successfully applied, the writer would state that, while acting as general manager of two large sulphite pulp mills, he directed the application of piece-work to all of the complicated operations of manufacturing throughout one of these mills, by means of elementary rate-fixing, with the result, within eighteen months, of more than doubling the output of the mill.

The difference between elementary rate-fixing and the ordinary plan can perhaps be best explained by a simple illustration. Suppose the work to be planing a surface on a piece of cast iron. In the ordinary system the rate-fixer would look through his records of work done by the planing-machine, until he found a piece of work as nearly as possible similar to the proposed job, and then guess at the time required to do the new piece of work. Under the elementary system, however, some such analysis as the following would be made :

Work done by Man.	Minutes.
Time to lift piece from floor to planer table...............	———
Time to level and set work true on table....................	———
Time to put on stops and bolts.............................	———
Time to remove stops and bolts.............................	———
Time to remove piece to floor....	———
Time to clean machine.....................................	———

Work done by Machine.	Minutes.
Time to rough off cut $\frac{1}{4}$ in. thick, 4 feet long, $2\frac{1}{4}$ ins. wide.	———
Time to rough off cut $\frac{1}{8}$ in. thick, 3 feet long, 12 ins. wide, etc.	———
Time to finish cut 4 feet long, $2\frac{1}{4}$ ins. wide....	———
Time to finish cut 3 feet long, 12 ins. wide, etc...........	———
Total......................	———
Add ——— per cent. for unavoidable delays.............	———

It is evident that this job consists of a combination of elementary operations, the time required to do each of which can be readily determined by observation.

This exact combination of operations may never occur again, but elementary operations similar to these will be performed in differing combinations almost every day in the same shop.

A man whose business it is to fix rates soon becomes so familiar with the time required to do each kind of elementary work performed by the men, that he can write down the time from memory.

In the case of that part of the work which is done by the machine the rate-fixer refers to tables which are made out for each machine, and from which he takes the time required for any combination of breadth, depth, and length of cut.

49. While, however, the accurate knowledge of the quickest time in which work can be done, obtained by the rate-fixing department and accepted by the men as standard, is the greatest and most important step towards obtaining the maximum output of the establishment, it is one thing to know how much work can be done in a day, and an entirely different matter to get even the best men to work at their fastest speed or anywhere near it.

50. The means which the writer has found to be by far the most effective in obtaining the maximum output of a shop, and

which, so far as he can see, satisfies the legitimate requirements, both of the men and the management, is the *differential rate system of piece-work.*

This consists briefly in paying a higher price per piece, or per unit, or per job, if the work is done in the shortest possible time, and without imperfections, than is paid if the work takes a longer time or is imperfectly done.

51. To illustrate: Suppose 20 units or pieces to be the largest amount of work of a certain kind that can be done in a day. Under the differential rate system, if a workman finishes 20 pieces per day, and all of these pieces are perfect, he receives, say, 15 cents per piece, making his pay for the day $15 \times 20 = \$3$. If, however, he works too slowly and turns out, say, only 19 pieces, then, instead of receiving 15 cents per piece he gets only 12 cents per piece, making his pay for the day $12 \times 19 = \$2.28$, instead of \$3 per day.

If he succeeds in finishing 20 pieces, some of which are imperfect, then he should receive a still lower rate of pay, say, 10 cents or 5 cents per piece, according to circumstances, making his pay for the day \$2, or only \$1, instead of \$3.

52. It will be observed that this style of piece-work is directly the opposite of the ordinary plan. To make the difference between the two methods more clear: Supposing, under the ordinary system of piece-work, that the workman has been turning out 16 pieces per day, and has received 15 cents per piece, then his day's wages would be $15 \times 16 = \$2.40$. Through extra exertion he succeeds in increasing his output to 20 pieces per day, and thereby increases his pay to $15 \times 20 = \$3$. The employer, under the old system, however, concludes that \$3 is too much for the man to earn per day, since other men are only getting from \$2.25 to \$2.50, and therefore cuts the price from 15 cents per piece to 12 cents, and the man finds himself working at a more rapid pace, and yet earning only the same old wages, $12 \times 20 = \$2.40$ per day. What wonder that men do not care to repeat this performance many times?

53. Whether coöperation, the differential plan, or some other form of piece-work be chosen in connection with elementary rate-fixing, as the best method of working, there are certain fundamental facts and principles which must be recognized and incorporated in any system of management, before true and lasting success can be attained; and most of these facts and prin-

ciples will be found to be not far removed from what the strictest moralists would call justice.

54. The most important of these facts is, that MEN WILL NOT DO AN EXTRAORDINARY DAY'S WORK FOR AN ORDINARY DAY'S PAY ; and any attempt on the part of employers to get the best work out of their men and give them the standard wages paid by their neighbors will surely be, and ought to be, doomed to failure.

55. Justice, however, not only demands for the workman an increased reward for a large day's work, but should compel him to suffer an appropriate loss in case his work falls off either in quantity or quality. It is quite as important that the deductions for bad work should be just, and graded in proportion to the shortcomings of the workman, as that the reward should be proportional to the work done.

The fear of being discharged, which is practically the only penalty applied in many establishments, is entirely inadequate to producing the best quantity and quality of work ; since the workmen find that they can take many liberties before the management makes up its mind to apply this extreme penalty.

56. It is clear that the differential rate satisfies automatically, as it were, the above conditions of properly graded rewards and deductions.   Whenever a workman works for a day (or even a shorter period) at his maximum, he receives under this system unusually high wages ; but when he falls off either in quantity or quality from the highest rate of efficiency his pay falls below even the ordinary.

57. The lower differential rate should be fixed at a figure which will allow the workman to earn scarcely an ordinary day's pay when he falls off from his maximum pace, so as to give him every inducement to work hard and well.

58. The exact percentage beyond the usual standard which must be paid to induce men to work to their maximum varies with different trades and with different sections of the country. And there are places in the United States where the men (generally speaking) are so lazy and demoralized that no sufficient inducement can be offered to make them do a full day's work.

59. It is not, however, sufficient that each workman's ambition should be aroused by the prospect of larger pay at the end of even a comparatively short period of time. The stimulus to maximum exertion should be a daily one.

56

This involves such vigorous and rapid inspection and returns as to enable each workman in most cases to know each day the exact result of his previous day's work—*i. e.*, whether he has succeeded in earning his maximum pay, and exactly what his losses are for careless or defective work. Two-thirds of the moral effect, either of a reward or penalty, is lost by even a short postponement.

60. It will again be noted that the differential rate system forces this condition both upon the management and the workmen, since the men, while working under it, are above all anxious to know at the earliest possible minute whether they have earned their high rate or not. And it is equally important for the management to know whether the work has been properly done.

61. As far as possible each man's work should be inspected and measured separately, and his pay and losses should depend upon his individual efforts alone. It is, of course, a necessity that much of the work of manufacturing—such, for instance, as running roll-trains, hammers, or paper machines—should be done by gangs of men who coöperate to turn out a common product, and that each gang of men should be paid a definite price for the work turned out, just as if they were a single man.

In the distribution of the earnings of a gang among its members, the percentage which each man receives should, however, depend not only upon the kind of work which each man performs, but upon the accuracy and energy with which he fills his position.

In this way the personal ambition of each of a gang of men may be given its proper scope.

62. Again, we find the differential rate acting as a most powerful lever to force each man in a gang of workmen to do his best; since if, through the carelessness or laziness of any one man, the gang fails to earn its high rate, the drone will surely be obliged by his companions to do his best the next time or else get out.

63. A great advantage of the differential rate system is that it quickly drives away all inferior workmen, and attracts the men best suited to the class of work to which it is applied; since none but really good men can work fast enough and accurately enough to earn the high rate; and the low rate should be made so small as to be unattractive even to an inferior man.

64. If for no other reason than it secures to an establishment a quick and active set of workmen, the differential rate is a valuable aid, since men are largely creatures of habit; and if the

piece-workers of a place are forced to move quickly and work hard the day-workers soon get into the same way, and the whole shop takes on a more rapid pace.

65. The greatest advantage, however, of the differential rate for piece-work, in connection with a proper rate-fixing department, is that together they produce the proper mental attitude on the part of the men and the management toward each other. In place of the indolence and indifference which characterize the workmen of many day-work establishments, and to a considerable extent also their employers ; and in place of the constant watchfulness, suspicion, and even antagonism with which too frequently the men and the management regard each other, under the ordinary piece-work plan, both sides soon appreciate the fact that with the differential rate it is their common interest to coöperate to the fullest extent, and to devote every energy to turning out daily the largest possible output. This common interest quickly replaces antagonism, and establishes a most friendly feeling.

66. Of the two devices for increasing the output of a shop, the differential rate and the scientific rate-fixing department, the latter is by far the more important. The differential rate is invaluable at the start, as a means of convincing men that the management is in earnest in its intention of paying a premium for hard work ; and it at all times furnishes the best means of maintaining the top notch of production; but when, through its application, the men and the management have come to appreciate the mutual benefit of harmonious coöperation and respect for each other's rights, it ceases to be an absolute necessity. On the other hand, the rate-fixing department, for an establishment doing a large variety of work, becomes absolutely indispensable. The longer it is in operation the more necessary it becomes.

67. Practically, the greatest need felt in an establishment wishing to start a rate-fixing department is the lack of data as to the proper rate of speed at which work should be done.

There are hundreds of operations which are common to most large establishments ; yet each concern studies the speed problem for itself, and days of labor are wasted in what should be settled once for all, and recorded in a form which is available to all manufacturers.

68. What is needed is a hand-book on the speed with which work can be done, similar to the elementary engineering handbooks. And the writer ventures to predict that such a book

will before long be forthcoming. Such a book should describe the best method of making, recording, tabulating, and indexing time-observations, since much time and effort are wasted by the adoption of inferior methods.

69. The term "rate-fixing department" has rather a formidable sound. In fact, however, that department should consist in most establishments of one man, who, in many cases, need give only a part of his time to the work.

70. When the manufacturing operations are uniform in character, and repeat themselves day after day—as, for instance, in paper or pulp mills—the whole work of the place can be put upon piece-work in a comparatively short time; and when once proper rates are fixed, the rate-fixing department can be dispensed with, at any rate until some new line of manufacture is taken up.

71. The system of differential rates was first applied by the writer to a part of the work in the machine shop of the Midvale Steel Company, in 1884. Its effect in increasing and then maintaining the output of each machine to which it was applied was almost immediate, and so remarkable that it soon came into high favor, with both the men and the management. It was gradually applied to a great part of the work of the establishment, with the result, in combination with the rate-fixing department, of doubling and in many cases trebling the output, and at the same time increasing instead of diminishing the accuracy of the work.

72. In some cases it was applied by the rate-fixing department without an elementary analysis of the time required to do the work; simply offering a higher price per piece providing the maximum output before attained was increased to a given extent. Even this system met with success, although it is by no means correct, since there is no certainty that the reward is in just proportion to the efforts of the workmen.

73. In cases where large and expensive machines are used, such as paper machines, steam hammers, or rolling mills, in which a large output is dependent upon the severe manual labor as well as the skill of the workmen (while the chief cost of production lies in the expense of running the machines rather than in the wages paid), it has been found of great advantage to establish two or three differential rates, offering a higher and higher price per piece or per ton as the maximum possible output is approached.

74. As before stated, not the least of the benefits of elementary rate-fixing are the indirect results.

The careful study of the capabilities of the machines, and the analysis of the speeds at which they must run, before differential rates can be fixed which will insure their maximum output, almost invariably result in first indicating and then correcting the defects in their design, and in the method of running and caring for them.

75. In the case of the Midvale Steel Company, to which I have already referred, the machine shop was equipped with standard tools furnished by the best makers, and the study of these machines, such as lathes, planers, boring mills, etc., which was made in fixing rates, developed the fact that they were none of them designed and speeded so as to cut steel to the best advantage. As a result, this company has demanded alterations from the standard in almost every machine which they have bought during the past eight years. They have themselves been obliged to superintend the design of many special tools which would not have been thought of had it not been for elementary rate-fixing.

76. But what is, perhaps, of more importance still, the rate-fixing department has shown the necessity of carefully systematizing all of the small details in the running of each shop; such as the care of belting, the proper shape for cutting tools, and the dressing, grinding, and issuing same, oiling machines, issuing orders for work, obtaining accurate labor and material returns, and a host of other minor methods and processes. These details, which are usually regarded as of comparatively small importance, and many of which are left to the individual judgment of the foreman and workmen, are shown by the rate-fixing department to be of paramount importance in obtaining the maximum output, and to require the most careful and systematic study and attention in order to insure uniformity and a fair and equal chance for each workman. Without this preliminary study and systematizing of details, it is impossible to apply successfully the differential rate in most establishments.

77. As before stated, the success of this system of piece-work depends fundamentally upon the possibility of materially increasing the output per man and per machine, providing the proper man be found for each job and the proper incentive be offered to him.

78. As an illustration of the difference between what ought to be done by a workman well suited to his job, and what is generally done, I will mention a single class of work, performed in almost every establishment in the country. In shovelling coal from a car over the side on to a pile one man should unload forty tons per day, and keep it up, year in and year out, and thrive under it.

With this knowledge of the possibilities I have never failed to find men who were glad to work at this speed for from four and a half to five cents per ton. The average speed for unloading coal in most places, however, is nearer fifteen than forty tons per day. In securing the above rate of speed it must be clearly understood that the problem is not how to force men to work harder or longer hours than their health will permanently allow; but, rather, first, to select among the laborers which are to be found in every community the men who are physically able to work permanently at that job, and at the speed mentioned, without damage to their health, and who are mentally sufficiently inert to be satisfied with the monotony of the work, and then, to offer them such inducements as will make them happy and contented in doing so.

79. The first case in which a differential rate was applied furnishes a good illustration of what can be accomplished by it.

A standard steel forging, many thousands of which are used each year, had for several years been turned at the rate of from four to five per day under the ordinary system of piece-work, 50 cents per piece being the price paid for the work. After analyzing the job and determining the shortest time required to do each of the elementary operations of which it was composed, and then summing up the total, the writer became convinced that it was possible to turn ten pieces a day. To finish the forgings at this rate, however, the machinists were obliged to work at their maximum pace from morning to night, and the lathes were run as fast as the tools would allow, and under a heavy feed.

It will be appreciated that this was a big day's work, both for men and machines, when it is understood that it involved removing, with a single 16-inch lathe, having two saddles, an average of more than 800 pounds of steel chips in ten hours. In place of the 50-cent rate that they had been paid before, they were given 35 cents per piece when they turned them at the speed of 10 per day, and when they produced less than 10, they received only 25 cents per piece.

80. It took considerable trouble to induce the men to turn at this high speed, since they did not at first fully appreciate that it was the intention of the firm to allow them to earn permanently at the rate of $3.50 per day. But from the day they first turned 10 pieces to the present time, a period of more than ten years, the men who understood their work have scarcely failed a single day to turn at this rate. Throughout that time, until the beginning of the recent fall in the scale of wages throughout the country, the rate was not cut.

81. During this whole period the competitors of the company never succeeded in averaging over half of this production per lathe, although they knew and even saw what was being done at Midvale. They, however, did not allow their men to earn over from $2 to $2.50 per day, and so never even approached the maximum output.

82. The following table will show the economy of paying high wages under the differential rate in doing the above job :

COST OF PRODUCTION PER LATHE PER DAY.

Ordinary system of piece-work.		Differential rate system.	
Man's wages	$2 50	Man's wages	$3 50
Machine cost	3 37	Machine cost	3 37
Total cost per day	$5 87	Total cost per day	$6 87
5 pieces produced.		10 pieces produced.	
Cost per piece	$1 17	Cost per piece	$0 69

The above result was mostly, though not entirely, due to the differential rate. The superior system of managing all of the small details of the shop counted for considerable.

83. There has never been a strike by men working under differential rates, although these rates have been applied at the Midvale Steel Works for the past ten years ; and the steel business has proved during this period the most fruitful field for labor organizations and strikes. And this notwithstanding the Midvale Company has never prevented its men from joining any labor organization. All of the best men in the company saw clearly that the success of a labor organization meant the lowering of their wages, in order that the inferior men might earn more, and, of course, could not be persuaded to join.

84. I attribute a great part of this success in avoiding strikes to the high wages which the best men were able to earn with the differential rates, and to the pleasant feeling fostered by this system ; but this is by no means the whole cause. It has for years been the policy of that company to stimulate the personal ambition of every man in their employ, by promoting them either in wages or position whenever they deserved it, and the opportunity came.

A careful record has been kept of each man's good points as well as his shortcomings, and one of the principal duties of each foreman was to make this careful study of his men, so that substantial justice could be done to each. When men, throughout an establishment, are paid varying rates of day-work wages, according to their individual worth, some being above and some below the average, it cannot be for the interest of those receiving high pay to join a union with the cheap men.

85. No system of management, however good, should be applied in a wooden way. The proper personal relations should always be maintained between the employers and men ; and even the prejudices of the workmen should be considered in dealing with them.

The employer who goes through his works with kid gloves on, and is never known to dirty his hands or clothes, and who either talks to his men in a condescending or patronizing way, or else not at all, has no chance whatever of ascertaining their real thoughts or feelings.

86. Above all is it desirable that men should be talked to on their own level by those who are over them. Each man should be encouraged to discuss any trouble which he may have, either in the works or outside, with those over him. Men would far rather even be blamed by their bosses, especially if the "tearing out" has a touch of human nature and feeling in it, than to be passed by day after day without a word, and with no more notice than if they were part of the machinery.

The opportunity which each man should have of airing his mind freely, and having it out with his employers, is a safety-valve ; and if the superintendents are reasonable men, and listen to and treat with respect what their men have to say, there is absolutely no reason for labor unions and strikes.

87. It is not the large charities (however generous they may

be) that are needed or appreciated by workmen, such as the founding of libraries and starting workingmen's clubs, so much as small acts of personal kindness and sympathy, which establish a bond of friendly feeling between them and their employers.

88. The moral effect of the writer's system on the men is marked. The feeling that substantial justice is being done them renders them on the whole much more manly, straightforward, and truthful. They work more cheerfully, and are more obliging to one another and their employers. They are not soured, as under the old system, by brooding over the injustice done them; and their spare minutes are not spent to the same extent in criticising their employers.

A noted French engineer and steel manufacturer, who recently spent several weeks in the works of the Midvale Company in introducing a new branch of manufacture, stated before leaving that the one thing which had impressed him as most unusual and remarkable about the place was the fact that not only the foremen, but the workmen, were expected to and did in the main tell the truth in case of any blunder or carelessness, even when they had to suffer from it themselves.

89. From what the writer has said he is afraid that many readers may gain the impression that he regards elementary rate-fixing and the differential rate as a sort of panacea for all human ills.

This is, however, far from the case. While he regards the possibilities of these methods as great, he is of the opinion, on the contrary, that this system of management will be adopted by but few establishments, in the near future, at least; since its really successful application not only involves a thorough organization, but requires the machinery and tools throughout the place to be kept in such good repair that it will be possible for the workmen each day to produce their maximum output. But few manufacturers will care to go to this trouble until they are forced to.

90. It is his opinion that the most successful manufacturers, those who are always ready to adopt the best machinery and methods when they see them, will gradually avail themselves of the benefits of scientific rate-fixing; and that competition will compel the others to follow slowly in the same direction.

91. Even if all of the manufacturers in the country who are competing in the same line of business were to adopt these methods, they could still well afford to pay the high rate of wages demanded by the differential rate, and necessary to induce men to work fast, since it is a well-recognized fact the world over that the highest-priced labor, providing it is proportionately productive, is the cheapest; and the low cost at which they could produce their goods would enable them to sell in foreign markets and still pay high wages.

92. The writer is far from taking the view held by many manufacturers that labor unions are an almost unmitigated detriment to those who join them, as well as to employers and the general public.

The labor unions—particularly the trades unions of England—have rendered a great service not only to their members, but to the world, in shortening the hours of labor and in modifying the hardships and improving the conditions of wage-workers.

In the writer's judgment the system of treating with labor unions would seem to occupy a middle position among the various methods of adjusting the relations between employers and men.

When employers herd their men together in classes, pay all of each class the same wages, and offer none of them any inducements to work harder or do better than the average, the only remedy for the men lies in combination ; and frequently the only possible answer to encroachments on the part of their employers is a strike.

This state of affairs is far from satisfactory to either employers or men, and the writer believes the system of regulating the wages and conditions of employment of whole classes of men by conference and agreement between the leaders, unions, and manufacturers to be vastly inferior, both in its moral effect on the men and on the material interests of both parties, to the plan of stimulating each workman's ambition by paying him according to his individual worth, and without limiting him to the rate of work or pay of the average of his class.

93. The level of the great mass of the world's labor has been, and must continue to be, regulated by causes so many and so complex as to be at best but dimly recognized.

The utmost effect of any system, whether of management,

social combination, or legislation, can be but to raise a small ripple or wave of prosperity above the surrounding level, and the greatest hope of the writer is that, here and there, a few workmen, with their employers, may be helped, through this system, toward the crest of the wave.

DISCUSSION.

Mr. H. L. Gantt.—One cannot read Mr. Taylor's admirable paper on "A Piece-Rate System" without realizing that it contains vastly more than the title suggests. It is really a system by which the employer attempts to do justice to the employee, and in return requires the employee to be honest.

His method of fixing rates by elements eliminates, as nearly as possible, all chance of error, and his differential rates go a long way toward harmonizing interests of employer and employee.

It was my good fortune to work for a year as his assistant in this work, and I fully agree with him as to the effect on the men. They improve under it, both in honesty and efficiency, more than I have ever seen them do elsewhere. Realizing that substantial justice was being done, and that to do their duty was to follow their own interest, it soon became a matter of habit with them.

The greatest obstacle in the way of adopting this system is that the man in charge of the rate-fixing department must be a man of more than ordinary ability, and should have had a very wide experience. To err in fixing a rate has a very bad effect upon the men, who should never have reason to think that the element of "guess" occurs in their rate. It is therefore only in a comparatively very large establishment, where a capable man can be employed to give his time to this work, or in a very small one, where the superintendent can give it his personal attention, that the plan is entirely applicable.

His idea of a hand-book on the speed with which work can be done, similar to the elementary engineering hand-books, is one which is bound to interest all progressive engineers, and I hope that he will see that his predictions about such a book do not fail.

In paragraph 15 he states that a clerk in the factory is the particular horror of the old-time manufacturer. Why is this? In many cases the manufacturer is a shrewd and successful man, and if so, why has he not seen the advantage of using a clerk in connection with his foreman?

This takes us back to the advantages of a system. No matter how successful a system may be in one shop, modifications are always required to make it equally successful in any other. No shop should be run to suit the demands of a system, but the system must be modified to suit the demands of the shop. No system is a success unless it makes work go more smoothly and cheaply, and ultimately makes the proper running of a shop independent of any particular man.

The fact that most ready-made systems fail in almost all of these respects makes the shrewd, old-style manager fight shy of them, and regard any approximation to them as a needless expense.

To pay men what they are worth requires that we keep accurate records of their work, and as the foreman is too valuable a man to be used as a clerk, he should have this work done for him, and be free to give his entire time to his men and the work.

Finally, the ideal system must be automatic and self-contained. It must be so simple as to appeal to those working under it, and should impose checks in such a way as to prevent or correct errors without the interference of the superintendent, or of any one not directly connected with doing the work under it, and, above all, it should be free as possible from "red tape."

Mr. F. A. Halsey.—Mr. Taylor's paper points out that in cases where the machine cost exceeds the wages paid, a piece-rate which increases with the output may be compatible with reduced cost, as the output advances. Simple as is the idea, it is, I must own, new to me, and it may be admitted at once that in such cases the advancing piece-rate is justifiable, *provided the maximum output cannot be obtained without it.* In the average case, however, where the wages paid exceed the machine cost, the condition no longer holds, and the advancing piece-rate would involve an increased cost, as an accompaniment of an enlarged output.

It was under the condition of a moderate tool cost that my Premium Plan (see vol. xii., page 755, of the *Transactions*) was devised, and its application, under a high tool cost, was not considered, the fundamental idea being that the workman's earnings *per piece* should decrease (though per day increase) as the output increased. By reference to my paper on the Premium Plan it will be seen that the need of different premium rates to cover different conditions was clearly recognized, and while such a development was not contemplated, it is plain that there is nothing to prevent making the premium rate so high as to give the workman a wage which increases faster than the output, *if the conditions are such as to make that course necessary* to secure the maximum output.

It thus seems to me that, while Mr. Taylor's plan is applicable only to the condition of high tool cost, the Premium Plan not only applies to the condition of low tool cost, for which it was planned, but to the condition of high tool cost as well. There are not many shops in which the maintenance of every tool costs more than the wages of its operator—the tools falling under that class being usually in the small minority. Mr. Taylor's system being economically applicable only to the larger tools, it would seem necessary, if the best results are to be obtained, to apply it only to such large tools, and use some other system for the smaller ones. With the Premium Plan, the same system, as has been shown, applies to all, and its advantage in requiring only one system of time and cost keeping against two, with Mr. Taylor's system, is apparent.

Is it clear, however, that a wage rate which advances faster than the output is necessary in any case? The only system which will endure is the one which pays the least possible per piece of product. The purpose of these systems is not, primarily, to pay high wages, but to produce cheap work, the adjustment sought being one which shall give the workman an increased wage *per day* in return for a decreased cost *per piece* of product. In my experience, a comparatively small premium will call out a workman's best efforts, provided the work is not too laborious, and the workman is *assured against future cuts in the rate.* Why should this not be the case with large and expensive tools as well as small ones, and, if true, why should the wages increase faster than the product, even on large tools?

Mr. Taylor's strictures on the piece-work plan' have my cordial approval, but what is the fundamental difficulty with piece-work? Simply that the output under it is always found to be larger than anticipated, and a rate which seemed moderate before trial is found to be excessive after trial. The workman's earnings, increasing *pro rata* with the product, soon get to be excessive, unless he has acquired wisdom and restrains himself. In Mr. Taylor's system, the earnings under an increase of product increase still faster than with piece-work, and the consequences of a too high rate would be even more serious than with piece-work. Wherein, then, does the superiority of Mr. Taylor's system over piece-work lie? *Not in the advancing piece-rate, but in the method of fixing rates.* If Mr. Taylor can determine the maximum output of the miscellaneous pieces of work comprised in the everyday operation of the average machine-shop, he has accomplished a great work, and the present paper should be followed at once by another, giving the fullest possible details of his method. It is this universal difficulty of determining the possible output which is at the bottom of the difficulties besetting the piece-work plan, and it was its contemplation which led the writer's thoughts to the Premium Plan. With that plan, the attempt to determine the possible output is abandoned. Present output is taken as the basis, and if the premiums offered for an increase are small, as they should usually be, no possible increase of output can carry the workman's earnings beyond reason. It is its extreme flexibility and the absence of danger of expensive errors of judgment which chiefly commend the Premium Plan, and while it is impossible to judge Mr. Taylor's method of fixing rates with the present knowledge of it, I must say that it is hard to conceive anything so simple or safe as the plan offered by me.

Still another point presents itself. When piece-work is introduced in place of day's work, the rate offered is usually less than the work previously cost. The workmen often object, as few of them know the real capacity of the tools, and the system is only introduced by the exercise of some coercion on the part of the employer. Nevertheless these first rates are eventually found to be too high, and a really large output is only reached after several successive cuts. Now, if the final output is to be determined at once by Mr. Taylor's method, and the rates fixed in accordance, is not still greater opposition on the part of the men to be expected? The maximum output is usually and necessarily a matter of growth. With Mr. Taylor's plan there must intervene a period of low pay. The outcome is uncertain to the workmen. They are full of distrust, and can they be blamed if they rebel? Right here, again, the merits of the Premium Plan are conspicuous. There is no cut at its introduction; on the contrary, present output is taken as the basis, and the workman is offered an increased wage if he will increase the output. The result is satisfaction from the start, and increasing satisfaction as time goes on. Nothing can be simpler, fairer, or plainer, and nothing can meet all the varied conditions more perfectly.

Mr. F. W. Taylor.—In Mr. Halsey's criticism of my piece-rate system, he very justly lays great weight on the elementary rate-fixing as the most important part of the system. An accurate knowledge of the quickest time in which each job can be done is the very foundation upon which the differential rate rests, and without this knowledge the whole system must fall to the ground.

Mr. Halsey is in error, however, in his assumption that my system of piece-work involves paying a higher price per piece than is paid under the ordinary system. On the contrary, with the differential rate the price will, in nine cases out of ten, be much lower than would be paid per piece either under the ordinary piece-work plan or on day's work. An illustration of this fact can be seen by referring to paragraphs 79 to 83 of the paper, in which it will be found that a piece of work for which the workmen had received for years, under the ordinary piece-work system, 50 cents per piece, was done under my system for 35 cents per piece, while in this case the workmen earned $3.50 per day, when they had formerly made, under the 50-cent rate, only $2.25 per day.

It is quite true that under the differential rate the workmen earn higher wages than under other systems, but it is not that they get a higher price per piece, but because they work much harder, since they feel that they can let themselves out to the fullest extent, without danger of going against their own interests in the long run. What I said in the paper was that the management could *well afford* to pay a higher price per piece, to insure the maximum possible output, not that it was necessary to do so. Mr. Halsey is right in saying that there is sometimes difficulty in introducing the differential rate, owing to the great and sudden increase in speed which is demanded of the workmen. This is particularly true of the first few cases in which the system is applied in a new establishment—*C'est le premier pas qui coute*—and much tact and skill is sometimes required to get the men to accept and work under the first rate. After the system, however, once has a start in a place, on however small a scale, the workmen are quite as quick to recognize its merits from their standpoint as the management are from theirs.

Mr. Halsey's is by far the best of the ordinary systems of piece-work, yet, even under his system, there still remains what to my mind is the very weakest point of all the ordinary systems, and what may be called, almost, the curse of modern industrial management, namely, *that it is for the workman's interest to* "*soldier*" *and go as slowly as possible on each new piece of work that comes along*, so as to get as high a price per piece as possible when piece-work first starts; and for this reason, even after piece-work has been inaugurated, under Mr. Halsey's plan, there is almost necessarily a great lack of justice in the prices fixed for different jobs, since the starting-point from which the first rate is fixed is unequal and unjust. Some of the rates may have resulted from records obtained when a good man was working close to his maximum speed, while others are based on the performance of a medium man, at one-third or one-quarter speed, and from this follows a great inequality and injustice in the reward of even the same man when at work on different jobs.

Other defects of Mr. Halsey's plan, and which are corrected by my system, are:

First. That it is slow and irregular in its operation in reducing costs, being dependent upon the whims of the men working under it.

Second. That it fails to especially attract first-class men and discourage inferior men.

Third. That it does not automatically insure the maximum output of the establishment per man and per machine.

Mr. John A. Penton.*—Although I am not a member of the Society, I want to thank you for the privilege of just saying a word. The paper we have just listened to and the presentation made by Mr. Taylor strike me as being perhaps the most remarkable thing of its kind I ever heard in my life. I do not wish to say anything about its merits, or demerits, if it has any. My knowledge of it is altogether too superficial to admit of anything of that sort; but I can sympathize with every word he said, for the reason that fortunately, or perhaps unfortunately, I was for five years at one time occupying the position of president of a very large organization, which would be called a labor organization, prominently identified with the iron business. With us, the treatment of this piece-work problem was something which, even now as I think of it, causes me to shudder and to feel a little nervous; and when I think of the problems which might be solved by this paper presented by Mr. Taylor—such a one, for instance, as was solved by the military at Homestead a year or two ago—when I think of all those things, and of the numberless

---

* Formerly President of the Brotherhood of Machine Moulders, present by invitation.

instances which occur almost every year, I feel that, as a workman, I want to congratulate Mr. Taylor and to say that his paper, I think, is a landmark in the field of political economy; and, as all our leading thinkers have devoted their time in the last few years to solving problems of that kind, I feel that the paper he has written is worthy of the greatest consideration at the hands of every employer, and at the hands, also, of the employee. It seems to me that every sentence, almost, might form a text for an article. It certainly enunciates a number of logical ideas, and I feel that I would like to go before the American Society of Mechanical Engineers, and, as a workman, testify to my feelings in the matter.

Mr. W. S. Rogers.—It is strange how we meet old faces once in a while. In 1883, in the State of Ohio, I had charge of men, and that identical plan of a differential piece-price came into my head. I was not near as old then as I am now, but I recognize, also, the fact that I am not talking to students now. I am talking to men who know more than I do of how to handle men. A very capable member of this association, who is now dead (Captain Minot), was a particular friend of mine, and I laid this plan before him. He said : " Do you believe in it ? " I said : " I think that is just the thing to fetch my shop right down to where it ought to be." He said : " Try it." He went by my shop to and fro to his, and he would stop occasionally and say : " Rogers, how is the differential working ? " At first I was enthusiastic. At the end of six weeks, he said : " Rogers, what do you think of the differential ? " I said : " Captain, I feel like a thief; it isn't honest. There are times when a man cannot turn out as much work to-day as he did yesterday, and it is not his fault; the fault lies sometimes in the foundry or elsewhere, and the man is not to blame, but I have got to live up to my rules and cut the price." " Well," he said, " I thought you would feel that way, and I have been feeling that way for you." Then I abolished it. At the Providence meeting, Mr. Halsey read a paper on the Premium Sharing Plan. I have tried it three times since. I have a friend of mine trying it. I am trying that in the shop where I am to-day, and it is simple and easy, and the men ask for it. You cannot give it to them fast enough, and you do not require a rate fixer. Now, as to cutting prices and cutting rates, I know an instance that occurred not long ago. A man took charge of a shop, and not ten days after he went there he slapped it on to

57

piece-work. To-day he is looking for another situation and the firm is cutting the men. You cannot pass to piece-work instantly, or anything else, until you thoroughly understand the whole situation; and you have got to throw your hobbies and ideas to the winds and be governed by what you find and the men you find. A short time ago a man applied at our place for work. I make it a point, if possible, to hire every man. He said he was a machinist. He asked what wages he would get. I said: "That depends on you; your rate will not be fixed for one week." I asked where he was from. He replied that he was glad to get away from a place where the differential system was in operation.

Mr. F. W. Taylor.—I must object to Mr. Rogers saying that he tried my system of piece-work; for, according to his own statement, he entirely omitted the vital part of my plan, namely, the elementary rate-fixing, without which the differential rate must, in most cases, prove a failure. He, however, says that he only tried differential rates for six weeks, which, in point of fact, is no trial whatever. If he had tried the plan for six years or even six months, and abandoned it, his experience might have some weight, but six weeks counts for nothing. Regarding his statement that his workman was glad to get away from my system, all that I need say is that about a thousand of the most intelligent, most prosperous, and contented workmen in the country are working there under this system, and a majority of these men have been in the employ of the company for more than ten years, without complaint about the system, and without a strike or even the talk of a strike. Can Mr. Rogers say as much regarding the workmen of any other steel works in the country?

Mr. Wm. Kent.—I am very glad that Mr. Rogers has attacked Mr. Taylor's paper. There are very few men who have the courage to do it. I hope there will be others who will rise up and attack it, and I know of no man stronger than Mr. Taylor to repel such attacks. He is just the kind of man to stand a good deal of hammering, but sometimes I think he may come out on top.

In regard to Mr. Halsey's plan, which Mr. Rogers has indorsed, I had the pleasure some years ago of indorsing it also, and I think I was possibly the first one to put it on trial, because Mr. Halsey had told me about it two or three years before he published his paper. So far as I know, the plan has been an entire success. But my opinion is that Mr. Taylor's plan is a little ahead. It is probably a little better, provided it is carried out with proper intelligence, by the right men, with proper sense of generous treatment of their workmen. I regard this whole question, which was started, possibly, by Mr. Towne, in his paper, then continued by Mr. Halsey, and now supplemented by Mr. Taylor's paper, as one of the most important questions, not only before this Society, but before the world to-day— the harmonizing of labor and capital; and this question is not to be settled by the opinion of the old-time mechanics, such as my young friend who has spoken. It is to be settled, after a profound study, by men capable of logical analysis, and by students of political economy, and I do not expect that we are going to introduce any of these systems, in any great degree, by the men who are now over fifty years of age, who have all their old-time prejudices; but I think it will be from such men as the one who presented those opening remarks, such as Mr. Gantt, a young man, a technical graduate, who has given some attention not only to workshop matters, but to political economy, and that such men will be the ones who will introduce this system in the long run. I hope to see this subject of workshop economics taught as an inductive science from actual statistics—statistics of tool cutting, of wages, of rates, in the modern method of studying political economy; that this science must be taught in our technical schools, and that our graduates will graduate, not with the knowledge of how to apply this system, but with minds trained to begin studying the system in practice, and gradually the proper system for our shops will be evolved. I heartily congratulate Mr. Taylor on the paper he has presented, and hope he will continue his studies for a great many years to come in this direction.

Mr. D. L. Barnes.—I would like to ask Mr. Taylor a question about a matter upon which he has not entered in his paper. How does he deal with the apprentice system? A good apprentice will often do as much work as a journeyman. Now, is he to get the same price? The temptation for the manufacturer is to use as many apprentices as possible. How are disputes about apprentices with labor organizations to be settled? That, to my mind, is the most important problem with which a manufacturer has to deal, when the work is such that an apprentice can do it.

The plan proposed by Mr. Taylor is applicable in a shop where the profit is great and where there is an unlimited amount of orders to work on. But suppose the contract price is fixed, and the orders are not very frequent, and the profits small; can a man afford to pay more for extra quality work than for what will pass as good work? It seems to me that the manufacturer can afford, under those conditions, to pay only one price, and that is to get work good enough to pass inspection, and how the differential rate system can be applied under those circumstances I do not see.

Mr. Taylor.—The answer to that is this : With regard to apprentices, in the first place, the Midvale Steel Company takes no regular apprentices, in the old-fashioned meaning of the term, but they do take a great many boys, young men, and even older laborers, and teach them trades, and when I was there I treated my apprentices or learners just as I would the other men. I let them earn all that they could earn, and I was delighted to have them do it. I do not care who turns out my work. So much work is worth so much money, whether done by an apprentice or by a man just tottering to the grave. With all due respect to Mr. Barnes, the apprentices or learners are not able to do, in my experience, anything like as much work as the first-class trained workmen are able to do, and under the differential rate system they must be content with the lower price per piece. They, however, always have the higher price per piece before them as a goal, to spur them on to become fast and accurate workmen, and the system has certainly worked admirably in this respect, since I should say that fully two-thirds of the skilled workmen of the place have been taught their trades right there in the steel works.

As to the second matter referred to by Mr. Barnes, namely, the applicability of the differential rate to a shop which did not have sufficient work to completely occupy all of its tools ; if the differential rate system involved paying a higher price per piece than is paid under other systems—that is, if you had to pay with the differential rate actually a higher price for a piece than your competitors pay—then Mr. Barnes is perfectly right in saying that in a shop which runs slack of work this could not be done. As I have already explained in answering Mr. Halsey, however, in most cases where the differential rate is applied your actual piece-work rate is lower than your competitor's price is, so that you have the advantage not only of a larger productivity per tool, but also a lower price per piece.

Mr. Rogers.—Mr. Barnes touched on the apprenticeship question, and I want to air myself a little on that subject. It is a nice thing to sit here and talk on these subjects, but when we get into the shop, into the cold-blooded grind of practice, it is totally different. Now, I do not believe an apprentice has any business in the Midvale Steel Works any more than he has in the works where I am. An apprentice goes in and contracts with his employer, and the employer is to teach him the business. When an apprentice comes into our works, I cannot conscientiously arrange to have that man spend three months on the miller, four months on the vice, on the big planer, on the boring mills, teaching him how to run all those things and how to become a first-class mechanic. If I do, I turn that shop into an educational institution and the firm loses. If I put the man where he belongs and keep him there, and make him good at one particular point, I am dishonest toward him. He works three or four years, and his time is up. I cannot afford to pay him what a good mechanic is worth, and he goes to the next shop—in some other town. "Where are you from?" "So-and-so's steam-pump works," and the first day he is fired out for spoiling a job, and they say, That is the kind of work they turn out up there. The apprentice belongs only in a shop where he works to-day on a sewing machine and to-morrow on something else. Our shop is not a machine-shop; it is a factory, a manufacturing establishment, just the same as the Midvale Works, and an apprentice has no business in either.

Mr. Gustavus C. Henning.—I would like to add a few words in commendation of Mr. Taylor's paper, not because I have been an employer of labor, but simply because I have suffered from being in intimate connection with unsatisfied laborers. I found that, in shops where the old-fashioned piece-rate was in vogue, every time a man did a good piece of work his wages were cut down. They would induce a man to turn out the work on the plea that it had to go out in a hurry, and just as soon as his amount of work increased his rate was cut down, so that he was always kept to earn about the same amount of money per day. I remember one case where this had a very important effect on the character of the work. It was driving rivets. The men were driving originally about 2,500 steel rivets, with hydraulic riveters, by contract, but they earned so much money at the rate they were getting that before the next lot of similar work was contracted for a lower rate was offered, and the men had to drive 3,500 instead of 2,500. The first trouble that arose was that 90 per cent. of the rivets were not absolutely tight. Then the shop began to question the propriety of the inspector marking all the loose rivets, because most of them could only be shown to be loose by tapping them on both sides of the head, but if tapped on one side only they would rarely show a defect. Then the men were made to cut out this work at their own expense and put in new rivets, the shop paying for the new rivets, but the labor was found by the riveting gang, and they lost money. Then the power for driving the rivets was increased, improving the work very much. The men actually succeeded in running up their capacity to about 4,500 rivets per 10 hours, but there were so many loose ones in the work that the men, of themselves, discarded the use of steel rivets, although it was prescribed by the specifications, and used iron rivets, because they could be driven tighter. Then, when the objection was made that the contract called for steel rivets, heaven and earth were raised to prevent the reintroduction of steel rivets, and the work was shipped one hundred and twenty-six miles, with these wrought-iron rivets in place, and it was only after the severest fight that they were compelled to cut out about 3,000 iron rivets in the field and replace them by steel, simply to make the contractors understand that they would have to carry out their agreement. That was all caused by the piece-rate system. If such a system as this had been in use, such a thing could never have occurred. Those men were trying to do their best, but by doing their best they were compelled to work harder and were getting less and less pay; the work was inferior to what it was when the men were getting less pay and turning out less. I think, if such a system as Mr. Taylor here describes can be carried out on any work in hand, and arranged to suit the particular shop in which it is to be introduced, it would certainly improve the work, increase the capacity, and make the general relation between employer and employee a far more satisfactory one than it is in many of our works at the present day.

Mr. C. E. Bement.—I would like to ask Mr. Taylor a question or two. Do I understand that when the maximum day's work is fixed, it is never changed?

Mr. Taylor.—When, by the elementary rate-fixing, you have found out what a maximum day's work is, for instance, on a lathe or a planer, on a certain class of work, that rate is never changed until some new element enters the problem; that is, until you

have a distinctly new method of doing the work. If you invent a
new tool which will turn out more work, or if the machine heretofore used is materially improved or better speeded, etc., then the
rate is altered; but while the conditions remain the same as
originally, and after a careful and thorough analysis has been
made of the quickest time in which the job can be done, that rate
is never cut ; that rate remains permanent until a material change
takes place in the rate of wages paid throughout the country—
such a change, for example, as occurred very generally in the rate
of wages paid in 1893. At this time, the rate of wages paid
under differential rates was cut, and the men did not complain of
the cut. They saw the justice of it.

Mr. Bement.—Suppose, in ordinary piece-work, the same pains
was taken and the piece-work price was fixed on that basis,
wouldn't that be as just as your system? You fix a day's work
which you calculate is the greatest that the machine or man
can turn out. Now, suppose in an ordinary piece-work shop,
such as I am running, we fix a piece-work price based on a maximum day's work, why is not that as just a price, provided the
same pains is taken to fix it?

Mr. Taylor.—If you can once persuade your men that you are
really going to allow them to earn more than the usual standard
of wages no differential is essential; that is to say, it is not then
nearly as necessary as it usually is. I think I said distinctly in
the paper that, after your men are thoroughly in accord with
the management and you are all pulling together, it is possible to drop the differential rate without a great sacrifice of the
amount of your product, but even then you will make a sacrifice
of possibly 10, 15, or 20 per cent. of your product, because the
incentive of earning his differential is lacking to make each man
work to his maximum. The case is very much like running a
race—if there is no goal to reach, if each man can go at any
rate of speed to suit himself, they will not go as fast as they will
if they have got to get to the tape at a certain time, or else forfeit
their premium. That is the incentive of the differential rate.
What I did not speak of and what is of equal importance is, that
it spurs the firm to keep their shop in the best of order. Everything must be kept up in the finest state of repair, or the men cannot earn their differential rate, and I think, if possible, that this
indirect result of the system is a greater benefit to the firm
than the rate is itself.

Mr. Rogers.—This gentleman's question and Mr. Taylor's answer make the thing clear to me now. This differential rate is really a punishment inflicted on a man when he does not attain the high standard fixed—the maximum standard—in the quality of the workmanship. As long as he does that he receives no punishment, but when he fails, he is punished under the disguise of a differential rate.

Mr. Platt.—I would like to ask Mr. Taylor whether the price is set at what might be called the highest possible efficiency. For instance, in the case of turning tires, the rate is put down at 35 cents if 10 tires are turned, and at 25 cents if less than 10 are turned. Now, is 10 all that it is possible for a man to do, or would he ever get out 12?

Mr. Taylor.—The case referred to in the paper was not that of turning tires. In this case, however, I have known one man to get out 11 pieces in the whole course of years of work. That is the most that has ever been done in a day.

Mr. Platt.—Concerning the highest price, it seems to me that some have overlooked the fact that it is an advantage to the works to have the men turn out as much as possible, because it costs just as much for fixed charges, whether the tool turns out 5 pieces or 10. On page 879 of this paper, the "machine cost," which I suppose includes all kinds of fixed charges, is given at $3.37 per day. That is $33\frac{7}{10}$ cents on 10 pieces, and $67\frac{4}{10}$ cents on 5 pieces, a difference of $33\frac{7}{10}$ cents. That is a very good profit on some pieces. On that account, I think it is desirable to let the men know that you know how much it is possible to do. I have been on both sides of this question, and I do not take wholly either the side which Mr. Rogers takes or the side that Mr. Taylor takes. I must say that I lean a good deal more toward Mr. Taylor than toward Mr. Rogers. I never had any difficulty in instituting the piece-rate price.

Allusion has been made to apprentices. I had experience for a number of years with a "bonus" system, which worked admirably, and in which there was a prize—not a forfeit—in case the boy did his work properly. Starting in at 50 cents a day, we worked up to $1.25. We advanced wages every six months, and credited a bonus to those who did their work properly. At the end of four years, or whatever the time was, they were paid what had accumulated. If one came in two or three days before the term was up, and wanted a little of the bonus money, it was

refused, and they were told, " If you come here after six o'clock on
the last night of the apprenticeship you will get your bonus, but
if meanwhile you maliciously spoil a machine, you will forfeit the
whole bonus." The consequence was that the boys took their $100
or $145 when the time was up, put some of it in the savings bank,
and became some of the best workmen in the shops. I do not
believe there is anything in this world that we work for except
reward and the fear of punishment.

Mr. J. L. Gobeille.—This paper is especially interesting, since
our moral responsibility toward those in our employ is so prominent a feature of this discussion. In a certain concern, twenty
men were displaced by that number of women, the output of both
being practically the same. Now, the average pay of these women
was much less, perhaps one-half what the men had earned.

While we are discussing ethics and morals, the question comes
to me whether it is right to put those women in at the highest
rate they had previously earned, and thus save an equal sum for
the department, or whether they should have been paid, as Mr.
Taylor paid his apprentices, equal pay for equal work. Apprenticeship, by the way, is a back number and a lost art, except in
shops in small country towns, and they do not pay the same rate
as men get per unit of work.

Seriously, I believe the "woman question" will be prominently
before the Society in a few years. In a little while women will be
running all the lighter tools in machine-shops and factories. This
is certainly coming. I am doing it and others must come to it.

Believing that our first duty is to the workman, and profit on the
investment a secondary consideration, what discrimination, if any,
shall we make between men and women, without, perhaps, in
every instance taking the high moral ground that Mr. Rogers
esteems so important in running a factory?

Mr. J. F. Holloway.—Feeling that I may possibly claim a place
in that class known as old-time mechanics, I would like to say a
few words on the matter under discussion. It certainly does commend itself to all thoughtful and well-meaning persons, that there
should be some method provided by which workmen could obtain
a better rate for what they do, and, at the same time, that proprietors should make more money out of it. Whenever that can
be accomplished, it certainly will be a long step in advance. It
seems to me that, in these latter days, so many combinations and
so many differences have come up that it is exceedingly difficult

to see how this may be brought about. The changed conditions in manufacturing, especially in the line of manufacturing with which most of us are connected, that of machinery, are so different from what they were years ago that they have brought in new complications. As Mr. Gobeille has well said, he doesn't know where the apprentices are to-day. I myself hardly know where you will find apprentices. When Mr. Rogers and I were boys, the apprentices were in small shops. The machine shops of this country were individual shops; they were owned by the man who operated them, or by a small partnership, and the apprentice had the privilege, the inestimable privilege, of living in the family, of getting up in the early morning and making the fire, milking the cow, and taking care of the horse, before he went to work in the shop. There was a certain community of feeling, in those days, between the boys in the shop and the master, which I think passed away when machine-shop owners became corporations, when they were managed by a board of directors who never saw the workmen, who knew nothing of them, individually, and, as I fear, cared less.

It is unfortunate in many ways that there should have been that sort of a diversion of interests, that sort of almost antagonism which has grown up in these latter years between workmen and their employers, and often for the reason that they do not know who their employers are. They know the superintendent of the works, and they know their foreman, and they have a slight acquaintance with the paymaster, through the medium of their check number, but over and beyond that they do not know who they work for. They never come in contact with the owners, and that sort of human contact which is so essential to good feeling, as Mr. Taylor has well observed, is not now prominent. The directors look only at the balance sheet. If the affairs of the company have been well managed, or the state of the market has been such as to enable them to show good balance sheets, then there is nothing said; but if unfortunate contracts have been made, or if the market prices have gone down and the balance is on the wrong side of the ledger, the directors, meeting in solemn conclave, say, Well, we have got to cut the workmen, and they do so; and in doing that there has grown up, as I say, a sort of antagonism between workmen and employers which is exceedingly unfortunate for both. If any way can be devised by which this can be remedied, it will be certainly an advantage to each. So far as the intent of the paper is concerned, and so far as the many good things in it are concerned, I heartily commend it, and I am very glad, indeed, to have listened to it. I am very glad, indeed, to know that there are gentlemen in the profession of engineering who are thinking and studying about the social side of these questions, and I am in hopes that something may come out of it which may be of mutual benefit. There are other elements which have come into existence in latter years which have been, I think, equally harmful. Among them are organizations, ostensibly for the benefit of the workman and possibly in some ways truly so. In many instances they have assumed to do the workman's thinking. They have assumed to take care of the workman, as they say, but unfortunately, in many cases, the men who have thus assumed to take care of the workmen are not the men who should have been put in the place of leaders, and it is, unfortunately, often for this reason that strikes arise, that divisions take place. There has grown up a feeling that one man shall have the same pay as another man, irrespective of his skill, experience, or industry. I think that is unfortunate, because it detracts from the energy and from the industry and from the ambition of a good man. These associations, which I am quite willing to believe were intentionally well-meant, and designed for the welfare of the workmen, compel certain things which I am certain do not in the end conduce to their advantage, because it brings all men to one lower level. No matter how good workmen they may be, no matter how industrious they may be, no matter how ambitious they may be to get a home for themselves and their family, they are tied down to one common grade and they are controlled often by one person, so that the individual liberty of the workman to-day is wanting.

As to the matter of apprentices and as to the matter of pay that they may get, I would say that the work of to-day is done largely by special machinery. I can hardly agree with my friend Mr. Rogers in his suggestion, elsewhere made at this meeting, that we should do away with all engine lathes, and throw them into the scrap heap; but it is true that the special machines of to-day largely supplement the industry and the intelligence of the workman. A bright young fellow, without any previous mechanical training, can go into almost any establishment and go on almost any machine, and with industry and application he can in a very short time do just as much as a skilled workman on that machine. In fact, the term skilled workman is now a very indefinite term. He may be a skilled workman on a slotting machine, or a shaper, or milling machine, but the true skilled workman, whom you could send anywhere to do anything, and who could accomplish it with few or no tools, is sadly wanting. So I can hardly see how you can manage the apprentice part of any system so long as there are no longer any apprentices to apply it to.

Mr. Chas. H. Norton.—I do not feel competent to discuss this paper, although my sympathies are with Mr. Taylor, and I believe his sympathies are with the right in this matter. About the apprentice question—Mr. Rogers says that apprentices have no business in a prosperous shop; that we cannot make money and run an educational institution; that is the way I interpret him. Now, if you were in my office I could show you a picture of some 60 or 80 apprentices; that picture was taken in their lecture-room, and the concern they worked for is probably the most prosperous machinery concern in the world. It is managed mostly on the day-work system, but the personal element of the manager has probably most to do with it. If our educational institutions could "*bring up*" mechanics, and educate into them the right personal elements to fit them to manage workmen *as men*, as Mr. Taylor says, such ability on the part of managers will bring success with any reasonable plan. The concern I refer to is the Brown & Sharpe Manufacturing Company, employing at one time 1,200 men. They have got 60 or 80 apprentices, and those apprentices are apparently happy, and they take a good deal of pride in their institution; as you see them in their lecture-room every week and somebody to talk to them there—in the establishment or from outside—you will see that they are enjoying it and they are learning something. And that concern is probably making as good a profit as any machinery concern in the world, and the profit is coming along with that "educational institution."

Mr. W. R. Warner.—There are quite a number of large manufactories where the apprentice system has been very successfully carried out. The firm in which I am interested often receive letters of application for positions from East and West and all around, and it is not a rare occurrence for the letter to begin with the statement that the writer served an apprenticeship with the Brown & Sharpe Company or with the Pratt & Whitney Company, and the fact is that that is the best recommendation that these young men can have. Being able to state that fact is equivalent to securing them work, and as a result it is very seldom that a person makes application to our shop who has ever learned a trade in those companies, because they have employment continually ; they do not get out of a job, and when they wish to change, all they have to do is to write to this, that, and the other firm, and work is offered them at once. Now, I am familiar with the system to which Mr. Norton has referred with the Brown & Sharpe Company, and also with the Pratt & Whitney Company, and I want to say that if a census of both those concerns were taken, you would find that nearly all the foremen or managers or chief draughtsmen were apprentices for those companies. This is an illustration, and pardon me for making it a personal one. The firm in which I am interested has as its superintendent a young man who learned the trade with us. We have as our chief draughtsman a young man who learned the trade with us. We have as our leading foremen, all through the establishment, young men who learned the trade with us. They are better than any we can hire. Just a word of encouragement for those apprentices. Take the Brown & Sharpe Company or the Pratt & Whitney Company. They supply their draughting-room with their best apprentices. It is a special reward of merit for any apprentice to secure entrance into the draughting-room. As a result these concerns never go outside to hire draughtsmen, because they have those among their own men who know their methods of construction, who understand all their system, and that is more than any outsider can possibly understand. A few weeks ago we needed a draughtsman. The superintendent said he was going to look over the young men in the shop and find who was the best one. Never for a moment did he think of going outside and hiring a draughtsman. But he went among the best workmen, and picked out one who was the most efficient when he was in the draughting-room. When we want a boy in the draughting-room, first beginning to trace drawings, and make blue-prints, and finally designing, we find the best boy who has made the best record, intellectually and morally and every other way, in his work in the shop, and as a special reward of merit that fellow is put in the draughting-room and given six months there. If he uses his opportunities he will, by the time he finishes his apprenticeship, be not only an excellent machinist, but a draughtsman and designer, and many such are being turned out every year in these large concerns down East. If you go among the shops in Chicago or the Western States you find in almost every one of them a few Pratt & Whitney men and a few Brown & Sharpe men. They have left the parent concern with the education they received there, and they are taking these leading positions in those large manufacturing concerns in the West. Now, most of those men I have referred to have not received a technical education. Doubtless, all would have succeeded better had they received a technical education. In a shop I know well, a young man who came from the woods of Maine is now superintendent, and has had under him for two years a professor of civil engineering who has taught in the colleges for twelve years, and still he has been under this backwoods boy, getting less than half the salary he receives, simply because, with his technical education, he has not come up to the standard which this other one had attained without it. I ought to qualify this remark simply to say that I do not in any way undervalue the technical education, but I state this to show how young men who came up from the ranks have, in spite of that drawback, gained ground every year, and come forward and developed qualities for commanding men, qualities for working out difficult engineering problems. One of the most important of those qualities is the qualification for managing men, and it is one department which I believe all colleges in the future will organize, with special methods. The colleges teach the rules in the books, they teach the engineering rules, but one of the most important things for any young man to learn is diplomacy, executive ability. It may all be summed up, perhaps, in those two words. Now, he can learn that in a large establishment like Pratt & Whitney's or Brown & Sharpe's, but never could he learn that in a college. It is one of the elements and qualifications which is most important and most essential in the education of any young engineer. I am glad to tell Mr. Rogers that these large companies down East are still keeping up the apprentice system, and the companies throughout the country are receiving good superintendents, who come from Brown & Sharpe and Pratt & Whitney and other similar institutions.

Mr. F. W. Taylor.[*]—I am much surprised and disappointed

---

[*] Author's closure, under the Rules.

that the elementary rate-fixing has not received more attention during the discussion. No better evidence could have been produced, however, of the crude and elementary state in which the art now stands, of determining the time to do work and of fixing rates, than that only one member of the engineering Society which is in the closest touch with the manufacturers of the country should have most briefly referred to the matter, while thirteen engineers have discussed at length the less important matter of what kind of piece-work to use.

I am, nevertheless, most firmly convinced that the question of scientific rate-fixing must occupy more and more of the attention of manufacturers in the future. Competition will force the subject upon them.

I think that this will prove a most fruitful field for investigation for young engineers in the future.

HISTORY OF MANAGEMENT THOUGHT

An Arno Press Collection

Arnold, Horace Lucian. **The Complete Cost-Keeper.** 1901

Austin, Bertram and W. Francis Lloyd. **The Secret of High Wages.** 1926

Berriman, A. E., et al. **Industrial Administration.** 1920

Cadbury, Edward. **Experiments In Industrial Organization.** 1912

Carlson, Sune. **Executive Behaviour.** 1951

Carney, Edward M. et al. **The American Business Manual.** 1914

Casson, Herbert N. **Factory Efficiency.** 1917

Chandler, Alfred D., editor. **The Application of Modern Systematic Management.** 1979

Chandler, Alfred D., editor. **Management Thought in Great Britain.** 1979

Chandler, Alfred D., editor. **Managerial Innovation at General Motors.** 1979

Chandler, Alfred D., editor. **Pioneers in Modern Factory Management.** 1979

Chandler, Alfred D., editor. **Precursors of Modern Management.** 1979

Chandler, Alfred D., editor. **The Railroads.** 1979

Church, A. Hamilton. **The Proper Distribution Of Expense Burden.** 1908

Davis, Ralph Currier. **The Fundamentals Of Top Management.** 1951

Devinat, Paul. **Scientific Management In Europe.** 1927

Diemer, Hugo. **Factory Organization and Administration.** 1910 and 1935

Elbourne, Edward T. **Factory Administration and Accounts.** 1919

Elbourne, Edward T. **Fundamentals of Industrial Administration.** 1934

Emerson, Harrington. **Efficiency as a Basis for Operation and Wages.** 1909

Kirkman, Marshall M[onroe]. **Railway Revenue.** 1879

Kirkman, Marshall M[onroe]. **Railway Expenditures.** 1880

Laurence, Edward. **The Duty and Office of a Land Steward.** 1731

Lee, John. **Management.** 1921

Lee, John, editor. **Pitman's Dictionary of Industrial Administration.** 1928

McKinsey, James O. **Managerial Accounting.** 1924

Rowntree, B. Seebohm. **The Human Factor in Business.** 1921

Schell, Erwin Haskell. **The Technique of Executive Control.** 1924

Sheldon, Oliver. **The Philosophy of Management.** 1923

Tead, Ordway and Henry C. Metcalfe. **Personnel Administration.** 1926

Urwick, L[yndall]. **The Golden Book of Management.** 1956

Urwick, L[yndall]. **Management of Tomorrow.** 1933